IGNITING
Within

A Hands-On Healer's Tips for
Awakening to Your Highest Self

CINDY SIMPSON JURADO

CONTENTS

Courage is to tell the story of who you are with your whole heart.

With Love
Cindy

Dedication

I dedicate this book to those who have entered this earthly plane
sensing that there's a greater intelligence—far greater than our own.
A Divine existence that speaks for itself, exceeding all labels of race,
religion, nation, or anything else that serves to separate or confine us.

We are here as awakening spirits born with Divine
wisdom, eternal truth, and connection with the galaxies
and all matter. Together, we are co-creating history.

Through our energies of passion, compassion, and the drive to evolve,
we are here to heal ourselves and help others to do the same.

We are embodiments of God, our creator, and His universe.
We respect His power by illuminating ourselves through
self-mastery, ultimately co-creating His legacy.

May this book, in a small way, reflect God's living and guiding
spirits, as well as our immense love and gratitude for the healings
and supernatural experiences that are beyond measure.

I thank you in advance for taking the time to detach from this
world, giving yourself the internal healing you deserve♥...

Shhhh! LISTEN.

CHAPTER 1

How Did I Get Here?

"Reincarnation: The belief that on the death of the body,
the soul (in time) transmigrates to, or is born again, in
another body." —*Collins Concise English Dictionary*

"God's ways are higher and better than our ways."—*Isaiah 55:9*

"And the Holy Spirit is with us to teach us to wake in Christ,
who is the way, the truth, and the life." — *John 14:6*

At the age of five, I found myself sitting under a beautiful deciduous tree on a hot summer's day in the city of Edmonton, Alberta. Instantly, a strange sensation came over me. I looked around and felt like I couldn't recognize anything or anyone. It was as if I were seeing everything for the first time. A dramatic shift in consciousness had just occurred—I felt like I'd been dropped from the sky and into this so-called physical body on this strange new earthly plane.

Oddly enough, an indigenous-looking woman stood at a distance, snapping photographs and smiling at me. "Say cheeeeese, Cindy!" she instructed me.

While she seemed to be in the flow of things and to know exactly why she was there, I, on the other hand, was confused. I looked around in wonder at the trees, the earth, the sky. I had no answers as to what any of it meant. In fact, to this day, I have no memories prior to the age of five.

"How did I get here?" I asked the woman who was taking photographs, as I continued to look around and take in the setting.

"What do you mean, how did you get here?" the woman chuckled. "Say cheeeeese for Mommy!"

Shortly after that experience, I was diagnosed with life-threatening asthma. It was almost as if the diagnosis was the obvious outcome of having been dropped into this body, into this family, into this alien world.

Thankfully, there was a hospital just up the road, so I had several episodes of running to and from the emergency room and being given endless prescriptions for inhalers. My life took on a surreal aspect, as I found myself living in oxygen tanks for months on end. My mother would sometimes watch over me with a combination of love and worry, and other times, she drowned her sorrows in alcohol. I missed a great deal of school and fell behind, although the medical ward at the hospital was kind enough to offer me my lessons, along with the other sick children, to hold me over until I was discharged.

When I returned home, I felt that I had so much energy to release, but my condition left me weak and limited. I often found myself wistfully looking out at the neighborhood children as they climbed trees and played hopscotch. I watched people walk their dogs and gazed at the pollen as it drifted off the petals of blooming flowers.

The woman whom I now knew was my mother shook her head as she saw me dreamily looking out the window. "You know you can't go out there, Cindy," she said. "The pollen could activate an asthma attack."

The lung disorder I had was such that inflammation caused my bronchi to swell and my airways to narrow, which created immense difficulty breathing. An asthma attack often felt like I was drowning in a deep swimming pool, with nobody around to save me. The medical team at our hospital had warned us that asthma like the kind I had could never be cured...although there was a slim chance I could grow out of it in the years to come—but with no promises. From what we'd been told, Western medicine could only do so much for me.

I recall one night in particular, when I was taken over by utter helplessness as my shortness of breath turned into wheezing and a complete constriction of my throat. Wide-eyed, I did my best to cry out; immediately, my dad came into my room and grabbed me, running down the block to the emergency room with me in his arms. I could practically feel my soul escaping my body as they slapped the oxygen mask onto my face.

I remember the experience of watching my dad as he himself gasped for air, his face red from exertion and breathlessness after having run so fast. I felt frail and somewhat guilty as I watched him. I knew how much he had sacrificed for me over the last two years. And by this time, my mother was also in constant fear after having watched me battle these random outbursts.

It was as if none of us could rest easy, considering that my last breath could be just around the corner. However, because I was so tired of being sick, I had no fear of death if it chose to knock on my door. Reflecting on my childhood, I recognize that even at that tender age, I knew I was never alone. I always felt as if I were surrounded by universal support, even when the adults in my life felt helpless when it came to protecting me from my illness.

And as my dad rushed me to the emergency room and I felt my breath fading away from my body, I was aware that my body was not yet ready for death.

Despite the drawbacks of my asthma, I believe that the question I asked myself at the age of five, "How did I get here?" began my journey back to spirit and seeded the ground for miracles yet to come.

I would later understand that when the soul is placed into the body, it has already come prepared with a clear agreement as to the type of human experiences it will have and the life lessons that one needs to learn in order to prepare for the next step in our evolution. Although we are not always conscious of these lessons, the soul is always looking for opportunities to open us up and to help us to grow and heal ourselves and one another.

In retrospect, being diagnosed with life-threatening asthma may have been a karmic contract, linked to a past life, that needed releasing. We are reborn to experience the vast veils of existence and to complete a Heavenly cycle of Divine missions that enable us to experience oneness and to create "everlasting life" here on earth. So even our suffering has a purpose, but we need not hold onto it forever.

In this book, I share my own personal journey of self-discovery and how the universe conspires behind the scenes to help us remember that there's more to life than what meets the eye. Each of us has the right to live our lives with a heartfelt purpose. We live in an "earthly classroom" where our lessons are meant to lead to healing. In fact, healing is in our very DNA. When we overcome the hurdles that face us, our life lessons lead us to the next stages of our soul's evolution.

In these chapters, I shine some light on the synchronicities and supernatural experiences that have marked my life, in the hope that they will shed light on your path of awakening. Many of us don't have answers to the question of how we got here and where we came from...but one thing is for sure: We need to live our lives in the present moment and be the best we can be by engaging purposefully with the world, so that we can reconnect with our origins at the end of our days and bring with us all the knowledge and soul connections we gained on the earthly plane.

My inspiration for writing about miracles and synchronicities was brought on by receiving prophetic downloads for myself and others that brought forth questions I was asked by clients who came to me for healing and consolation. Many of them were in 9-to-5 jobs that left them feeling depleted and unhappy. They had lost hope in the idea of a better life. They did not clearly know what their purpose was, but some soul-driven impulse within them had the desire to find out—and they were led to me. They were just waking up to their spiritual selves; although they didn't always know what the signs were pointing to, they understood that perhaps there was more to life than what they'd always believed or been told.

While my early sense of being dropped into this world never completely dissipated, and always kept me at a remove from my surroundings, I enjoy connecting with people from a bigger-picture perspective. When people share their troubles, I remind them that there is more to life than what is visible to the naked eye. Many of the stories you will read in this book are stories I've shared with others: stories of miracles, healing, love, and hope. As an intercessor who often prays on behalf of or over others to that the answers they are seeking will eventually come to them, I've seen physical ailments sometimes dissipate.

Infertility or even suicidal thoughts are often healed. I am accustomed to help-ing ignite people on their spiritual journeys. Sometimes, this might happen overnight—in a dream vision, or right from the healing bed. Or it may take several weeks or even months. But invariably, it happens. I personally don't have control over the outcome—God does. I am, as we all are, employed by Him in some shape or form.

I know from experience that through our learning and our spiritual evolu-tion, we have the power to ignite one another. We have the power to co-create paradise here on earth, as long as we are willing to listen to the spiritual guid-ance that is always ours to claim.

Although many of the stories in this book are rooted in Christianity, do not be fooled; the lessons are universal and transcend religion. Many people find themselves stuck in religious dogma, limited by the Church's mandates and ideas about hell, Heaven, sin, and God. This creates a sense of separateness. Your intuition will demonstrate the truth, so be sure to honor it. Spirituality offers us a window into understanding the vastness of God. God is utterly limitless, and so are our souls; when we wed religion with spirituality, we are able to see this.

However, Christianity offers a number of valuable parables that help to shed light on the experiences that many of us recognize in today's world. We live in what the Book of Revelation refers to as the "end times." We may find chaos surrounding us; political regimes are crumbling, people are at war with each other, and the earth is in a state of upheaval. Depending on your perception, it may look dire, but the truth is, those of us who are awakening spiritually are being prepared for a new earth. This so-called chaos is Mother Earth's way of cleansing herself in Divine order, and it's a blessing in disguise for generations to come. Everything will work itself out according to a greater plan.

While religion might chalk this up to Jesus resurrecting to judge the living and the dead, our karmic attachments will be our ultimate judge and jury. If we are not aware of the higher power that is guiding us to take stock of our lives and let go of our attachments, we will not integrate the lessons and pass on to the next level of our evolution. Instead, we will be doomed to repeat the cycle of suffering; we will simply be swallowed by the patterns of self-sabotage and sorrow that are so characteristic of the world today.

I encourage readers to step outside of judgment, fear, and dogma, and to think more broadly. Whether or not Christianity is your reference point, just know that Christ is true abundance. Life itself is vast and just as mysterious, so religion and spirituality need not be in conflict or overly complicated. Through the parables of Christianity, you will find that the fundamental message is one of love, oneness, compassion, forgiveness, and healing.

Thankfully, every single one of us holds the sacred temple of God within us. We each carry our own Christ self, together. God created us all to be at our best and has offered us various ways to connect with Him and His universe. There are many techniques and practices (including meditation with prayer) that can help us expand our inner knowledge in partnership with His universe. We can also begin the process of deep self-inquiry. For example, who's in your close circle of relationships? How are you maintaining these relationships? Are they draining or energizing you? Are there changes that need to be made in your lifestyle and your way of thinking? Are your thoughts and beliefs bringing you greater joy, peace, and awareness—or are you going through life on autopilot?

Many spiritual teachers who have experienced a near-death experience (NDE) talk about the "life review" that we all receive after our physical death, wherein we come to comprehend our most valuable lessons from that lifetime and also get a chance to see where we could have done better. We need not wait for death to experience such a review. We can obtain a new lease on life and receive the second chance we all yearn for.

When you are on the path of awakening, synchronicities, deja vu are bound to occur. And prophetic (psychic) abilities heighten, while seemingly random symbols or celestial universal nudges show up to try to get your attention. It's the creator's way of paving the path to a greater calling for you. However, those who refrain from seeing these universal messages with an open mind are usually blinded by their ego, pride, karma, doubt, stubbornness, and lower thought vibrations. Or perhaps their souls are not yet ready to be awakened and to remember their true identity. But this resistance creates struggle, which can generate health issues, addictions, and even unexpected tragedy. When we deny the call of the soul and the universe's desire for us to awaken, we often find ourselves engaging in behaviors and going down paths that are not in alignment with the soul self.

If you have found yourself in this position, then it's time to *accept* (learn from the lesson), *release* (let go and let God), and *surrender* (to the higher power, our creator). Do not let tragedy or strife instill fear in you. Instead, better yourself by seeing your trials from a positive perspective, allowing strength and courage to defeat any contamination that you allowed into your space. As one door closes, another always opens—and it's usually the better one in most cases. We must remind ourselves that during life's greatest storms, we still have our Divine heritage as sons and daughters of God. Silence your mind, expand your heart, find comfort in allowing yourself to heal in full forgiveness, and speak to the mountain with true love—and it, too, shall move.

This book is meant to heal your inner child—the one who knows there is so much more to life than this, and who longs to be lifted from his or her wounds to experience exactly what it means to be a child of God. Together, we can come to see that there is so much more to life than illness, suffering, or the unfulfilling 9-to-5 where you can be replaced in an instant. We can listen to our souls and be more mindful of the nourishment we take into our bodies and the people with whom we surround ourselves. We can surrender to God (creator) and recognize His signs in our lives. In sincerely asking for universal help, we will find balance, peace, and harmony within ourselves.

The surrounding energy for this book is now. All around us, there are more portals to awakening than ever before. It is customary for angels to appear in human or celestial form in order to bring awareness and hope to people everywhere. This is important, because we are in the midst of a remarkable shift that has been in effect since 2012. Through research and first-hand experience, I've learned what must be done in order for humans to raise their vibration and integrate the lessons that will enable us to evolve to the next level. So you can consider this book not just a collection of inspiring stories but a manual for raising your vibration while healing to ascend to the next level of our evolution.

Everything and everyone is orchestrated in Divine order. All of our challenges and rewards are interconnected with our soul contracts and assigned to us from the throne of Heaven. We are connected to a mighty energetic pow-erhouse, a source much greater than our own—which we ALL have access to.

We are never alone.

If you are reading this book, it's likely that your soul and the Divine order have orchestrated its placement in your hands to help you reconnect with your true self and grasp the understanding of oneness among others who are also on the same path—so that, together, you can find solace on your journey toward a new earth.

CHAPTER 2

How My Lungs Were Naturally Restored

"Jesus told us that His Spirit would live in us and upon Him, and we would do greater works." —*John 14:12*

"And He healed them all." —*Matthew 12:15*

I n 1981, at the age of seven, I was still battling my "no cure" respiratory condition. My mother stepped up to help me, although she'd had little education. She was also dealing with the consequences of early childhood trauma, during which she was molested by the Catholic priests who'd been responsible for taking her and other children away from their families so that they could be "properly" educated in convents.

I recall my grandmother sharing the tragic history of the First Nations families who'd been torn apart by this system. "Damn Ottawa separated our families!" she'd declare as she raised her fists and clenched her teeth in anger and disappointment. She also dwelled on the dysfunctionality of our great great grandfather, Governor-in-Chief Sir George Simpson of the Hudson's Bay Company during the period of its greatest power, 1820 to 1860. He was notorious for being the British Viceroy who had sired at least 11 children by at least 7 women, only one of whom was his own wife. Knowledge of his exploits had created a hush of separation among our families, and it still lingers today.

Although my mother had lost her faith in Catholicism, she was steeped in her belief in God. Her Catholic upbringing merged with her indigenous roots, and while her life was difficult and growing up in the convent system had been torture, my mother never lost her intrinsic faith in spirit.

In contrast, one side of my father's family was German and devout in their ways. I recall visiting my paternal grandmother, who would retire quietly to a corner of the room after dinner to read her Bible every night. I always found this fascinating, as neither my mother nor my father raised me in the church. However, signs of God were always around, and even when I went to bed at night, I would clasp my hands at the foot of my bed and bow my head to pray.

Please, God, send me a cure for my asthma. And make it so that my mother and father don't have to worry so much.

Overall, on top of the fact that my illness made my early childhood difficult and often painful, my family life was unstable. Because my mother's sorrow had led her to become an alcoholic, I was often left alone at an early age. When my mother was out on drinking binges, I was left to take care of myself if my father was on a business trip. Often, I would be lucky if I could even find a Kraft dinner, a slice of bread, or cereal with milk in the house.

Although I had five other siblings (two sisters and three brothers), we had different fathers (except for two, who shared a father). I was the youngest and didn't grow up around the others as much as I would've like to. One sibling had been put up for adoption, two others were raised by my maternal grandmother, and the others left home at an early age, in and out of foster homes and in the hands of social services. They eventually lived on their own—embittered against my mother and her inability to be a nurturing parent.

Although my parents were soulfully connected, they were never married and didn't really live under the same household. Although they often came together and my father was always a presence in my life, we didn't operate in the same way as a traditional family unit. I suspect that because my mother was rather young when she started having children, and my father had me late in his life, they didn't fully understand the responsibilities of raising a family or moving beyond their own selfish needs and desires.

At the same time, I knew that they were both doing their best. My mother, who was dealing with the fallout of early childhood trauma, was often suicidal. However, every time she felt that she'd given up hope and was ready to leave this world, something would happen and she'd receive a sign from God that helped her to stay the course. Once, an elderly gentleman knocked on the door to gift her with a Bible that he said he no longer needed; he was moving out, and he said he'd found it in one of his boxes. Dumbfounded, she accepted the gift and offered to give him money for it; he replied, "It's meant for you." She thanked him as she closed the door. After she closed the door, she peered out the window to watch him leave...but he was nowhere to be found. It was as if he'd vanished into thin air after delivering his message of hope.

My father lived with his mother while he ran his own business. Often, he would take me to my grandmother's house to cook me a meal, but given that nourishment was generally lacking in my life, my appetite was so small that I never really ate very much.

Although times were hard, whenever my parents did their best to be attentive and to take care of me, they were kind and supportive. I can also say that I admired my mother for never losing her strength despite her hardships. She was a soul fighter who understood that God the creator was so much greater than we could understand.

One day, she had the desire to demonstrate the deep spiritual reverence of our indigenous ancestors to me. She was convinced that we would find a cure for my illness in this way.

"Enough of this! I don't want to lose you, my girl," she said. She grabbed my hands, we hopped into my father's truck, and off we went.

"Where are we going, Mom?"

"We are going to the pilgrimage to have you healed," she replied with an earnest and determined look on her face.

I had no idea what she meant by that, but agreed all the same. We headed northwest on Highway 43 past huge expanses of historic lands, upon which farmers worked. As we passed pasture after verdant pasture, I began to relax. I appreciated the beauty and the quietude of this place. It was far different from the busy, noisy city life I'd grown so accustomed to.

I'd always found life in Edmonton disconnecting. My father would take a lot of road trips for his business, and sometimes my mother and I would accompany him but made a conscious effort to be close to a hospital if the inhalers didn't hold me over. So, from an early age, I was in awe of nature. The sense of peace I'd feel sitting and leaning against a tree (after a puff of my inhaler), my eyes closed, was indescribable. I wished I could be here all the time, held by the earth and the sky, connected to everything. It made me feel as if I could momentarily escape the chaos of the world, and detach from my identity and the life that had been given me.

As seconds turned into minutes, Mom and I approached a sign that read, "Welcome to Lac St. Anne Pilgrimage, Alberta Beach," and another adjacent to that that read, "Alexis Indian Reserve 133." As we parked off to the side, we were surrounded by traditional cone-shaped tents that looked like they were made out of buffalo skin, attached to wooden poles. I understood that these were what the indigenous people called teepees. As my mother explained to me, this place was a holy one for priests, nuns, and tourists from around the world. The waters of the Nakota Sioux were known as Wakame, or "God's lake," and were said to have healing properties. It had been said that the Sioux ancestors heard singing coming from the lake and understood it to be a message from God that revealed to them the water's healing powers. It was now the setting for one of the largest annual gatherings combining traditional and other beliefs among the indigenous people of the area. During the annual event, close to 30,000 people would come. Some would hobble to the lake's edge on crutches, and some would roll their wheelchairs until their feet were immersed in the cool water. Suitably, the left-behind crutches and canes were made into a shrine.

My mom grabbed my hand and pulled me toward one of the teepees when we were approached by three female elders with glistening long white hair whom I'd never seen before in my life. My mother repeatedly whispered in my right ear, "Know that God's real and He's going to heal you today, OK?"

The women didn't ask any questions. They immediately placed their hands on me and prayed. I took it that this was normal protocol for them, and that they were accustomed to performing hundreds of healings a week. Whatever the case, I immediately felt welcome, like I was being pulled into the radiant energy of love.

As I looked around, I noticed several other groups of people—some of whom were praying, and others of whom were being prayed over. But I immediately zoned them out and closed my eyes, until it felt as if the only people left were me and these three elders who were murmuring words of healing over me. I placed my head down as they continued to pray, and I simply accepted their blessings in silence. Then, suddenly, one of the women tapped me on my forehead, which made me collapse into my mother's arms ever so slightly. She comforted me and stroked my hair. I opened my eyes, somewhat disoriented, not truly understanding what had just taken place. Either way, we thanked the women for being of service.

Within minutes after the laying of hands, we were invited to a large teepee that enclosed a huge campfire. As my mother began talking to the other people gathered there, I wandered off to the fire pit that was within a few feet. The axe and the wood grabbed my attention. I was curious, and I wanted to help chop wood to feed the fire, too, so I grabbed the axe and began chopping. All this time, my mother was unaware of what was happening as her back was turned.

As I began chopping, I decided to hold the wood out with my left hand. When I lowered the axe, it cut through the wood effortlessly—and also sliced off the tip of my thumb!

I looked on in horrified alarm as the tip of my thumb dangled off my finger, blood rushing to the surface. "Mom, help!" I hollered.

She ran right over, accompanied by her friends, who helped by providing some bandages. As we were surrounded by a small crowd, my mom grabbed the tip of my thumb and gently placed it back on the rest of my thumb, adding pressure. By this time, it was bleeding profusely. She expertly wrapped my finger with a couple Band-Aids and then some bandages.

"Oh, she's going to need stitches for that!" some people murmured, concerned.

"Yes, you should see a doctor right away!" someone else said.

Because I was all bandaged up and it was already late, my mother thought we could wait until the following day, so we basically slept on the hope that my thumb would be fine until then. The following day, Mom said, "Let's replace the bandages before heading to the hospital."

As we slowly unwrapped them, our dread turned into astonishment. Remarkably, my finger had healed on its own!

If you were to look at my finger today, you would see the smallest remnant of a scar, but it would appear to you that nothing out of the ordinary had happened. I treasure the miracle that this scar left behind on my skin and the experience that took place around it, as a constant reminder that not only was my cut healed, but so was my life-threatening asthma.

Within 24 hours of our visit to the pilgrimage, the doctors could not explain how my thumb had healed itself, nor could they understand how my lungs were completely restored after they gave me a chest radiography. "It's as if there isn't any history of the respiratory condition of asthma," one of the doctors marveled.

Overall, my life changed completely overnight.

Considering my struggle for two whole years, I don't think it's possible to fully comprehend what had happened or how the healing had occurred. I don't feel the need to dwell on it, either, as I know that God works in mysterious ways. Of course, it took my mother to get to her own breaking point with my illness for us to make our visit to that place. I knew that she had her faith, but it was only this experience that made her a devoted believer in miracles.

Experiences we encounter create wisdom in which we take with us to further evolve in spirit. I believe that many of us would seek healing sooner if we truly knew that miracles were possible. Why continue to prolong our suffering and misery when we are gifted with the love of the unknown? What do we have to lose? Inviting our Divine team in and meeting them all the way is all it takes.

Let me reiterate that while both my parents were brought up in the Catholic church in two very different settings, they did not raise me in a religious environment—although we definitely prayed before meals and bedtime. So I was unbaptized, but I had still been healed. This is possible for everyone. Divine intervention can change our lives, merely when we ask for it.

Remember the powerful Biblical words, "Ask and you shall receive."

I often ask myself, "Where would I be if this miracle of healing hadn't taken place?" Well, all in all, I most likely wouldn't be here to tell this tale.

I leave you with a prayer of healing intention that you can use anytime you feel bereft of hope or are dealing with struggles that seem insurmountable: "Thank you, Guardian Angels, for protecting my aura field with an extra cloak of protection from all negative energies, and for sending messengers with the highest frequency of healing in these areas of my life: (be specific about what you are wanting to heal here). May I be led toward what is meant for me today and in my future, for my highest good."

CHAPTER 3

My Encounter with the Earthbound Soul

"Every experience is part of your life. You try to judge eternity by temporal happenings. You see in matter apparent confusion, but you don't realize that a Divine thread runs throughout all your lives."—Silver Birch

"God may give to you the spirit of wisdom and revelation in the knowledge of Him. The eyes of your understanding being enlightened; that you may know what is the hope of His calling, what are the riches of the glory of His inheritance in the Saints." *—Ephesians 1:17-18*

I t's been years since my healing occurred, but I know that it is a constant. Whoever is walking the earth plane is constantly in a state of healing. We're all healing on some level, in one way or another—physically, mentally, or emotionally. We are being given time to release any karmic attachments from our past lives and to bring spiritual awareness and knowledge in so that we can move forward. how to heal within moving forward.

For some people, the healing is more obvious. But even when it feels that it is not there, and all that befalls us is bad luck, healing occurs when we learn and grow from whatever we are experiencing. If a caregiver feels guided to care for others, this means they were gifted a strong soul, and that the experience (however painful) is a tremendous lesson for all involved. Everything that plays out is meant to be, and we are well rewarded for our actions, at least in a spiritual sense. Those who love from their heart, are willingly of service, and take the time to make a difference in the world are celebrated by spirit.

We are all works in progress that require mind, body, and soul maintenance. There is always some sort of illusion that is being tossed around within us internally and that we then bring into our reality. I know from my observations and through my own experiences that we can be our own worst enemy.

Reflecting back on my childhood, there were many periods of finding myself alone in a physical sense. I felt withdrawn from others of the human species in that I couldn't relate to people but continued humoring myself and others along the way and found comfort in it.

Moreover, in my family of origin, I didn't really have a voice. My father was head over heels for mom and would do almost everything in his power to keep her satisfied, but that didn't leave a lot of room for me. I know that my parents were simply doing the best they could, but their general m.o. was to let me know, on no uncertain terms, that my ideas and desires would always be secondary to what they needed and wanted. It was the proverbial treatment of children as objects to be seen and not heard.

If I spoke up for myself towards my mother (which wasn't that often), she would consider it "sassing back" and when my father was present, this wouldn't be tolerated. Once, she told him that I was being disobedient, at which point he removed his belt, hung me by my feet, and whipped me until I apologized and promised to never talk back to my mother again. That didn't take too long to put me in my place; after the first whip, I knew I would never cross that line again. My mother, on the other hand, would always recite to me her favorite of the Ten Commandments: "Honor thy mother and father." And if I didn't, God would punish me.

Does God punish? I thought to myself. In any scripture I read, He and His entourage were the most merciful beings and were always ready to help us upon request. It was up to us in "free will" to better ourselves in partnership, in spirit.

Although my parents preconditioned me in their fears, false beliefs, and lack mentality, they loved me the only way they knew how. I knew that in order to get along in my family, I simply had to listen to them and follow what they did. I found that it was easiest to simply detach from my emotions and what I felt. Honestly, I didn't believe that my own feelings ultimately mattered, although I would come out of this false belief during a spiritual awakening later in my life. I learned this: We heal when we don't give away our power to others who mistreat us. No one has power over you, unless you allow it—period.

As a child, I was a bit of a tomboy. I preferred to play marbles and hang out with boys rather than get caught up with girls and what seemed like female drama. At the same time, I was understanding toward others and tolerant of their ways. But I never truly had friends I could trust and share my feelings with. I found comfort in living a life of suppressed feelings, and having close friends didn't much matter to me. Often, I found it more peaceful to be alone than to be with others who were caught up in their fear-based illusions of self, as I already had enough of that in my own life.

As the youngest of five siblings, I carried a lot on my shoulders. Although I hadn't grown up with older siblings, I often found myself playing the part of "peacemaker" in our family. I attempted to do whatever I could to keep our family together. When my two siblings were in and out of foster homes, I would be the one to initiate the visit to see them with my mom; together, we would create games or ways to be able to bond despite the time restraints of the foster home, so that we could all enjoy each other's company. But being together wasn't exactly easy. My eldest siblings were understandably resentful toward my mother, as she'd never taken on the responsibility of being their parent but gave up custody to their grandmother and an adoptive family. All the same, my mother made an effort to check in on them throughout the years. Still, whatever joy we encountered in each other's presence was always short-lived.

When I was in elementary school, entering the fourth grade, I also went through some upheaval of my own. I was taken away from my mother for one year, during which I stayed with my father's sister, my auntie, for six months, and then with my older brother Greg, for another six months or so.

It wasn't really disruptive for me, though. I found it to be a blessing in disguise. My auntie taught me a number of things, from eating properly to being able to tell the time on an old-fashioned clock. And my brother, who was in his 30s at that time, was easygoing and fun. Overall, life in that year was more predictable, and more secure.

While my mother would seldom talk about this experience after she and I were reunited, I understood that what I was going through was simply another manifestation of her lifelong battle with self-destruction, dysfunctionality, and low self-esteem. As an aboriginal child, she grew up living in survival mode. Most people around her were accustomed to drowning their sorrows any way they knew how instead of learning to speak their truth and stand up in their own power.

However, as I know now, a lot of these people who have endured hardship in their upbringing mustered the strength to turn their lives around and become proactive about giving back to their communities and ending the cycle of pain and violence. They were determined to awaken and educated themselves, and ultimately found self-discovery through the conditions in which they were raised. Throughout their painful journey, they still honored their soul during the process. They used their obstacles to their advantage; in fact, the obstacles became forces that helped them move out of their comfort zone and develop their God-given talents, as well as share their journey to inspire others and teach them that they, too, could do the same. Their obstacles became a foundation that would allow them to give back to humanity, and to become the conscious generator of their own destiny.

My mother was a good soul for the most part, mostly when it benefited her and when it came to getting what she wanted. But quite often, I would witness her opening our doors to help someone in need of a place to stay for a short time by offering a home-cooked meal if we were blessed with some extra money. Or she'd lend a hand whenever there was a need placed in front of her path, which I feel has blessed her with miracles to this very day.

I learned a great deal from my mother, especially in those years that I ended up taking care of her through her alcoholism. I often found myself home alone, waking up to get ready for school, scrounging for food to prepare a lunch for myself, supplied from whatever welfare or food banks provided us. I developed grit and independence at an early age. I always lived in "survival mode" when she wasn't home or in an intoxicated state. And through it all, I knew that I wasn't alone. God and His Divine entourage seemed to be saying, "Not to worry—everything's under control."

By the age of 15, I entered high school. I was an average student who managed to keep up with my schoolwork the best way I knew how. I often found myself daydreaming and feeling disconnected from what was being taught, although I have to admit I felt a deep connection to some historical topics that were shared—one being the early fur trade (1500–1603) during which the British arrived in Canada and interacted with First Nations people for the first time. Who knew that I would be learning about my mother's people, and that my First Nations ancestors would be acknowledged for making history, despite the corruption, greed, and hardship that had afflicted them?

I still found comfort in my one-on-one quality time with my dad when he was in town, during which my mother would while her time away playing Bingo. We were not into watching television, but we enjoyed preoccupying ourselves outside of the Bingo hall as we waited for my mother. If it it was raining, I often would find myself sitting on my father's lap with my head resting on his heart, listening to the beats as if they was sharing an internal story of his future as they mixed with the background of raindrops that flew off the windshield or tapped on the roof over our heads. We sat in our truck listening to the radio on the lowest volume before we eventually dozed off. Sometimes we played card games inside or games like Red Light, Green Light outside. Children under the age of 16 were prohibited and not permitted beyond the front stairs that led into the hall, which were marked with red tape.

One night, as the Bingo games were coming to an end, my father glanced at his watch and suggested we start heading inside the hall. "They should be on their last bonanza jackpot game to end the night," he said.

We walked up to the red tape, where we stopped. We looked in at the players who'd bought into the jackpot, which looked like it was half empty at this point. "Do you see where your mom is sitting?" my dad asked.

I instantly spotted her and pointed her out in the crowd. "Right there!"

She was in the center of the building. The caller continued announcing the winning numbers. But for some odd reason, I had an internal pull to look at a man who was at the far back of the hall, close to a single rear exit door. He appeared to be unhappy. He was probably in his 30s, with shoulder-length textured hair. He was playing by himself at a table with his four bonanzas. I wondered why I kept glancing back and forth from him to my mother. I wondered if some innate knowing within me was telling me that one of them would win the game. But then, all of a sudden, someone else hollered, "Bingo!"

Disappointed that my mother didn't win, I felt the pull to again look at that same man. At that point, he banged his fists down on either side of his bonanzas, which immediately flew into mid-air. My jaw dropped and my eyes went big. I was utterly speechless, as if I were watching magic on TV. In a rage, he swung the bonanzas onto the floor, and I could hear the swish from the motion of his hands.

Wow, he must be super mad that he didn't win! I thought to myself.

Oddly enough, I noticed that no one around him reacted in the slightest; in fact, they were all in their own little world, going through the motions of exiting the rear door, since the game was finished and the winner had been declared. The man also got up to exit. But what I saw next shocked me. He literally walked *through* an older lady, who didn't show any reaction whatsoever. He bypassed the back door and headed straight through the brick wall. Once again, I seemed to hear the sound effects of his motion—this time, it was a strange staticky blip.

Caught off guard, I yanked on my dad's sleeve and urgently asked, "Did you just see that?!" Not even giving him time to respond, I quickly ran outside to the front of the building to see if I could catch the man. But as I looked all around the corner, he was nowhere to be found.

Both of my parents ran after me, confused. "What are you doing? Who are you chasing after?"

Out of breath, I began explaining what I'd just witnessed. My father simply went silent, while my mother brushed away what I imagined she thought to be my overreaction to the entire situation. "Just pray," she said. And given that neither of my parents seemed to be validating what I'd just seen, I instantly forgot all about it, as if it was just a TV show, as a child would.

Although I'd been trying to make sense of it, nobody had answers for me.

And despite my curiosity, something in my dad's silence and my mother's dismissiveness quickly shut off that curiosity.

In retrospect, I believe that my mother had always been intuitive. And from what I understood, so had an auntie on my dad's side. But the gift of intuition ran through my mother's lineage. My grandmother could always sense whether or not a storm was coming. "Make sure your teepee is hammered down!" she'd tell the others. At first, nobody believed her, but when the storms inevitably came, they went to her to seek her counsel and ask for her visions. My mother herself had been a witness to many miracles, which she pushed to the side over time because she worried that these moments were triggered by demonic powers. In fact, whenever anyone mentioned anything even slightly supernatural, she would quickly say, "I only believe in God," not considering that perhaps these were signs and blessings from God Himself. All this, despite all the healing experiences she'd lived through.

I believe that my mother's intuition, which came to her from her mother and possibly her mother before her, was passed down to me. At the age of 15, seeing the ghostly image of the man walking straight into a brick wall and vanishing was the first unexplainable thing I had ever encountered.

Today, I understand that there are portals to the Divine everywhere, and that the reunite the physical plane with the spiritual realm every second of the day. In fact, we physical beings could learn a lot from the spiritual realm of Heaven. Spirit beings deserve respect and to be heard through the veil that connects us all. We are all walking channels, whether we like it or not.

It's not unusual for people to see ghostly being, or for angels to appear out of the blue to help someone in a moment of crisis. We should not fear this. Spirit will find ways to help manipulate the situation at hand—whether through human messengers, tools of communication (such as the radio or a book), and the like. What we see or cannot see is based on what our soul wants us to experience in the external world. We may be able to recognize what others cannot for this reason alone.

Often, people who aren't ready to recognize the full truth of the situation in front of them will run away from it or avoid unforeseen or unfamiliar territory—until their soul forces them to align with the truth. Hence, there are differences in our individual soul's growth in each of our given journeys. Our states of consciousness allow us to exist at different levels of perception and at various vibrations—which brings confusion into any conversation among several people if they are not all on the same level. The effect is that it can sometime feel as if we exist in widely divergent realities.

What I know now about the Bingo experience is that my soul needed to witness this strange encounter. For some reason, I had to recognize that when we cross over into the spirit realm and come back in human form, we are what is known as "earth-bound." This man had crossed over, but somehow got caught in his earthly incarnation rather than moving into the Christ light. So when I saw him, although he had already transitioned, he was left feeling that he was still in his living human form! But just like him, we are all spirits in human form, having human experiences.

Spirit will come in periodically until you are ready to handle the full truth and perceive it for what it is. At that time, I didn't understand that what I was seeing was simply confirmation that portals between the spiritual and the earthly realm truly exist.

As an awakened soul with intention and purpose, I have come to realize that I am in "human form" and have been given another chance to cultivate more life lessons and to amplify my knowledge with spirit. Oddly, the earth-bound man had gifted me with a sample of the unknown, despite the fact that I would cast that experience out of my mind for years. Because I had seen it face to face, I could help to shed light on such experiences and bring awareness that such things are happening in and around us—and that we are not delusional, after all. We have the power to override false limited beliefs that stem from fear-based illusions, which keep us from seeing and knowing our truth.

No matter what you endure, know that you are always being Divinely guided, in Divine order, and fully supported—even more so when you are aligned with your true self.

CHAPTER 4

The Power of Connection

"Being deeply loved by someone gives you strength, while
loving someone deeply gives you courage."—Lao Tzu

"And we know that in all things God works for the
good of those who love him, who have been called
according to His purpose."—*Romans 8:28*

A few years passed, and before I knew it, I was a young 17 ½-year-old mother to be, wobbling around in my third trimester with my first-born daughter, Jasmine. At the age of 15, I met my first boyfriend, Vinny, who was nine years older than me. He was a kind and supportive young man, and both he and his family gave me a semblance of stability and love that I'd never truly experienced before. At the age of 16, I moved out of my house and into the one that he shared with his parents. We ended up renting their basement and began the process of building a life together...and with it, a family.

Although the relationship was serious from the very beginning, my pregnancy was unexpected. I discovered that I had an ovarian cyst, which led to emergency surgery. Miraculously, right after that event, I discovered that I was pregnant.

I'm not sure that any mother, no matter how old she is, is entirely prepared for the task of welcoming a baby into the world. But my experience with Vinny and his family was so comforting that I knew I would make it work. They were Chinese, and everyone was tightly knit and extremely sweet and supportive. They had a strong backbone of family values, and unlike the environment in which I was raised, Vinny's mother cooked for the entire household, always making sure that we were properly nourished and had what we needed. In my own home, I had been accustomed to going without meals or scrounging up my own dinners from whatever meager supplies we had in the kitchen cabinets.

I didn't have to worry about that anymore. I found comfort in the warm, home-cooked meals that I was served whenever I came back from work, and I loved the thoughtfulness that accompanied them. On top of that, Vinny himself was supportive, easygoing, kind, and family-oriented. And my entire first pregnancy was a blessed one, in that it was so easy. In the delivery room, upon dilation, three pushes was all it took. I was amazed when I first laid eyes on Jasmine, grabbing at her as I looked at the doctor. "Is this it?"

When Jasmine was born, I even witnessed her soul entering her body as she took her first breath. Her eyes lit up with a jolt, taking in the all the bright lights that surrounded us as she nestled into her body and the scenery. I could tell that she was deeply connected to the spirit realm, and her energy was attuned and sensitive—although I wouldn't realize the extent of her sensitivity until years later.

In this period of time, I sporadically saw my mother. Although my parents had never officially tied the knot, I knew that my mother longed for a more formal relationship. My parents remained friends and would come together on family occasions, but when I was still in elementary school, my mother met my stepfather and she ended up marrying him.

I never developed a meaningful relationship with my stepdad, because it was hard for me to accept him. I was close to my father because he was my blood, but I could never truly relate to my stepdad. He was French with a heavy accent, which didn't help much—and he was also a heavy smoker and drinker. A different character from me, altogether. My mother and stepdad would often get drunk together, so I didn't spend much time with them—which didn't bother me much at all, as long as my mother was happy. I simply let them do their own thing and came and went from school, always going straight to my room just to avoid them.

When I met Vinny and his family, I realized that I strongly gravitated toward Asian culture. I even came to understand a little Cantonese. They simply made me feel more at home and like I could actually raise a family in such an environment. In fact, after I had Jasmine, my mother-in-law stayed home with her while Vinny and I went to work most days, which freed up my soul.

Throughout this time, the hold that the spirit world had on me was never released, even though some part of me had forgotten all about my past supernatural encounters. The next encounter I had came during my third trimester of my pregnancy, when I wobbled up the stairs toward the family room—where everyone went to watch subtitled Chinese series and movies (most of which were way better than *Days of Our Lives*, that's for sure!). Just as I plopped down next to my sister-in-law, the phone began to ring, startling me.

I looked over at her. "Do you wanna answer this?" I asked. After all, I had my own cell phone for personal calls, and the landline wasn't one that I typically used.

She was so into the movie, I don't think she even heard me. On the fourth ring, I decided to answer it because whoever was on the other end seemed persistent.

I picked up the phone and heard an unfamiliar voice. The person sounded like they were an older Caucasian woman. "Oh, hello there, sorry to bother you...but is there an older gentleman there by the name of Bob, by any chance?"

I was slightly confused as I looked around. This was an Asian household, and there definitely wasn't anyone with the name Bob! "I'm sorry, but you must've dialed the wrong number, as there's no Bob that lives here."

An awkward silence crept in almost immediately, and I waited for her to respond. The silence was so prolonged that I began to feel a little uncomfortable at this point and wondered if I should just hang up.

Finally, the woman responded in a strange tone of voice, almost as if she were surprised. "Oh? I'm sorry, I guess I must have dialed the wrong number."

"That's OK," I responded before hanging up. I tried to return my attention to the Chinese film, but I couldn't concentrate. Something just wasn't sitting right with me. Odd as it seemed, something inside me was telling me to dial the number that the woman had called from. It was like my intuition was prodding me to investigate a little further...so I did.

I picked up the phone and pressed two buttons: "Last Caller," and then, "Redial." I waited patiently for the woman who'd called to answer. Admittedly, I had no idea what I'd say if she picked up. But I couldn't help but feel curious. Who was she, and why had she called? What was it about her that felt so mysterious? I wasn't sure if I'd get a straight answer, but some part of me wanted to know.

As I was contemplating what I might say if she actually picked up, someone who sounded like an older gentleman answered. "Hello?"

I don't know why, but I'd been so sure that the woman would answer that I simply looked at the phone in shock, not entirely sure what to say. But I allowed the words to just flow from me. "Ummm...sorry to bother you...but did an older lady just call from there asking to speak to a gentleman here, by the name of Bob?"

Like before, with the woman, an awkward silence took over and I waited for a response, all the while wondering what exactly was happening.

The man's voice sounded strained when he finally responded: "Well, my name is Bob...but as for an older woman, there isn't one around here anymore. I lost my wife a couple years ago."

An instant chill took over my body before I could even register his words. I didn't know how to react, or respond, for that matter. Somehow, I'd received a "phantom" call from this number...from someone who didn't even exist. It was completely eerie, and I was in shock.

I managed to say, "I'm so sorry for your loss, sir. I must have dialed the wrong number." I immediately hung up without waiting for a response or attempting to make sense of what had just happened. Eventually, I dismissed the memory altogether, just as I once had with my memory of the man who vanished at the Bingo hall.

Today, I feel differently. I surmise that my calling Bob shortly after receiving the call from the mystery woman was Heaven's way of sending a message to a grieving man.

Although I wish I would have been able to say something more to Bob, I understand that given my capacity at the time, I shut down to the reality of what was happening. And although I buried the importance of that encounter, it would eventually be unearthed and remembered later on my journey.

Perhaps Bob simply needed to hear that, in some way, his wife was sending him love and reassuring him of her continuity beyond the grave. Maybe she entered his dreams after that call, and gave him an even more explicit message. I don't know. I realize that part of the work of being a messenger for others is not knowing what your impact might be. All the same, I am sure that I ignited something—perhaps a spark of remembrance or solace. Now that the message had been delivered, they could both work it out on a soul level between them. I didn't need to know what happened next; and today, this story can simply be an illustration to help others who might be experiencing bereavement.

One thing I know for sure is that we are all tools and instruments for transformation. The spirit realm is always here to educate us; instead of shutting down occurrences like the one above as "unbelievable" or outside our comprehension, we can choose to move toward unexpected information with curiosity and openness.

Of course, at the age of 17, I wasn't awakened enough in my journey to better understand that situation, although this was another supernatural experience that my soul was ready to experience so that I could later reflect on it. Today, I know that Bob was probably mourning the loss of his deceased wife—who tried to reconnect to her living husband to let her know that she was OK in the realms beyond this one. In this case, for whatever reason, she chose me and the telephone as the vessel to reconnect yet again on this physical plane to offer him closure and healing...to let him know that they would once again reunite to finish their soul path here on this earth. After all, when we transition from this life to the next world, our souls are no longer limited in our dense bodies but are freer than ever before. And because love is the highest vibration in the universe, it continues, no matter what happens on the earth plane.

When we experience a loss in the family, it can bring about a great awakening. I know this from firsthand experience. So this felt like God's way of saying:

"There's more to life than what you think you already know." Seemingly minor events can alert us to our greater calling in life, and shake us awake.

We come into the world with a unique energy and capacity to make an impact on the world. And we also leave behind the imprint of our energy, just as the woman on the phone had left her impact on Bob. When we remember that we are all channels of love, we experience our lives in completely new ways.

And in my case, being chosen as the channel to convey a message to Bob was yet another breadcrumb along my path, letting me know what my purpose on this earth was.

CHAPTER 5

The Death of My Father

"I am absolutely convinced of the fact that those who once lived
on earth can and do communicate with us. It is hardly possible to
convey to the inexperienced an adequate idea of the strength and
cumulative force of the evidence." —*Sir William Barrett, F.R.S.*

"Ask, and it shall be given to you; seek, and ye shall find;
knock, and it shall be opened unto you: for everyone who
asks receiveth; and he who seeks finds; and to him who
knocks, the door will be opened."—*Matthew 7:7*

Years passed, and soon enough, I found myself the mother of two young and spirited girls: my older daughter Jasmine, an intuitive nine-year-old; and my younger daughter Jade, an easygoing and grounded three-year-old. Life as a mom was full of the predictable ups and downs, and the attendant joys and sorrows. As a family, Vinny and I were doing our best to connect and grow, to create a life worthy of our daughters.

At the time, I was working in retail and at a nearby clinic; when I wasn't working, I was spending time with my family. But in the last several years, things had taken a turn for the worse as it became clear that Vinny had a gambling problem. After I gave birth to Jade, I began to feel an increased restlessness. And although I loved Vinny, who had helped me to get out of an unhappy and unsustainable family situation, I was beginning to come into my own awareness and independence as a woman. I already knew that life could be easier, and I knew what a joyful family situation could look like...but now, an inexplicable part of me longed to reconnect to some part of my soul that wanted more.

I was a born nurturer, given that I'd grown up taking care of my mother for the most part, so this came very easily to me as a mom and a partner. I did my best to provide for my family, but deep down, I wasn't fulfilled. I had never left Alberta, and Vinny was not a fan of flying and long-distance travel, so while we went on road trips as a family, I longed to experience life beyond the confines of what I'd always known.

In the midst of this growing recognition that perhaps there was something more in store for me, I went on a road trip with Vinny and our two daughters. It was Father's Day 2002, and we were leaving Calgary and heading back home to Edmonton, which usually took us around three-and-a-half to four hours depending on the road conditions. That day, we were enjoying the hot sun and clear blue skies. Our eyes lingered on the birds flying overhead and the meadows filled with peaceful-looking cattle who stood and stared at us as they grazed. It was a gorgeous day, but in my emotions, a storm was brewing.

An unexplainable mood swing took over me. At some point, I began to cry uncontrollably. I didn't understand why, when I'd been so happy just moments before. But it felt as if I'd plunged into a bottomless well of sorrow, and I couldn't stop the tears from falling. Vinny looked over at me, concerned. "Are you OK?" I didn't know how to respond.

Just then, the car wildly jerked, which immediately caused us to pull over to the side of the highway and pop the hood to see what was wrong. We were confused, as the car was fairly new and we always had our vehicle inspected before taking any long-distance road trips, especially with our children in the car. But everything looked fine, so we went on our way, and the car seemed to be all right after that. My strange mood gradually subsided, and everything went back to normal as we continued on our way. Soon, all traces of that mysterious afternoon faded.

A couple weeks passed, and then I received an unexpected phone call from my mother. "I'm so sorry, my girl, but I'm calling to let you know that you lost your father two weeks ago on Father's Day," she said in a pained voice. It felt like the wind had been knocked out of me. My heart sank, and I simply collapsed to the floor, unable to comprehend my mother's words as the phone fell out of my hands.

Father's Day...the same day that the darkness had come over my happy thoughts and emotions, and our car mysteriously jerked. I knew beyond a shadow of a doubt that these had been signs from my father. It couldn't have been a coincidence! In fact, according to my father's DOA, which I would see a couple days later, the exact time of my experience coincided with that of his passing.

I wish I'd known right away, but this was life. My father had always been a private person. After my grandmother's death, he'd moved into a small apartment of his own in central downtown Edmonton, and the only times I saw him were when I initiated contact and offered to buy him lunch. For the most part, he lived as a single person without any family. His life was simple; beyond a bed and shower, there was little that he needed. And he was frugal to a fault.

One Christmas, I invited him to my house, but he ended up going to a convalescent home for seniors, where he enjoyed spending time with friends while receiving a free hot meal. I knew that my father had not been a smoker or drinker, but I assumed that his unhealthy eating habits and his extreme frugality had been responsible for his death. He avoided drinking plain water, never bought himself food, and if he did, it was usually cold sandwiches.

Eventually, the authorities notified me of my father's death, as well. I wondered why it had taken so long, so I called my auntie—the same one who had taken me in as a child so many years ago. I demanded to know why it took two weeks for them to contact me, and she candidly answered, "Well, because we didn't know for a fact that you were his biological daughter."

I was livid, but more than that, I was hurt. I learned that his body had been found in central downtown Edmonton in a men's washroom in City Hall, where he had apparently collapsed after a heart attack. His wallet had also been stolen, so it took days for the authorities to identify his body. By the time I'd discovered all of this, my father had already been cremated, so I didn't get a chance to say goodbye or keep any of his clothing that he wore that day as a keepsake. Still, I was grateful to carry his remains and organize a funeral service with a special eulogy on his behalf.

In 2004, two years after I was told the devastating news that I'd lost my father to a massive heart attack, my life was once more in a state of transition. I knew that I wanted to leave Vinny, and I was making the transition from selling our house to moving to Calgary to start a new life with my daughters. During that time, my dad visited me in a dream; as with most spiritual visits I experience, it was vivid and brief. It almost felt as if curtains had opened, revealing a film clip that held a symbolic healing vision. Who knew this was even possible! This experience linked me to the cosmos by night, somewhat similar to the late Edgar Cayce, who had been a gifted prophetic dreamer.

In the aftermath, I wondered why it had taken so long to connect with my dad's spirit after his death. I realized that my soul hadn't been ready to receive confirmation of his spirit's survival, as I was still in mourning. In addition, his spirit needed time to heal and reflect from the physical plane as his soul transitioned to the spirit realm, where he could learn how to manipulate my space so he could convey messages without my human ego getting in the way.

There he was, approaching me from a distance, glowing so radiantly. His skin was youthful, and he had a brilliant Christ-like glow around his face and body. He also had a peaceful smile on his face, the likes of which I'd never seen when he was alive. He placed his hands over his heart, and I knew through telepathic communication that he had died of a heart attack, which had taken his life and led him to transition to Heaven.

Then, the purest gold cross illuminated the scene. This was a little strange to me, as he'd never liked wearing jewelry when he was alive. As the cross materialized into its purest form, it felt so real, so sacred, and so beautiful.

Does Heaven even carry gold? I thought to myself. I knew it was a gift from God and that he was in great hands. When I woke up, my emotions of loss were evoked again, and sadness came rushing in. But there was also a profound ache of gratitude for my father's visit in spirit, and for the fact that he seemed to be offering me reassurance that he was still around, watching over me.

Years later, I would receive confirmation from spiritual mentors that after his passing, my father had become a master spirit guide for me. Of course, this is nothing either of us had been aware of when he was in human form, but after his death, he continued to send me signs and messages that came through as profound spiritual encounters.

That visit from my father gave me the strength to leave Edmonton for Calgary, as the single mother of two. It felt as if this confirmation was helping me to find the clean start that I desired...and to eventually manifest my future husband. It was almost as if my father was by side, helping to orchestrate and guide me through the entire experience...all the while reassuring me that it was OK to start over and that he was there for me in this new phase of my life.

In the past several years, I've recognized that while my father is certainly more aware than he was in life, he still has the same essential personality—he is humorous, truthful, and kind. However, his ego is gone, and the guard that was usually there in life has been let down. There is an authenticity that feels new to me...and yet I understand that it is the truth and core of his being, as he has shed his earthly worries and is now fully free to be himself.

I haven't encountered my dad in dreams very often—only three times in the last 15 years. But he continually lets me know that he's watching over me by sending me large random feathers, "dimes from Heaven," the news of my first grandchild, 7:11 on the clock or bus numbers, and even songs we used to sing together as a family on the radio when I was in elementary school.

The second time that my father came to me in a dream, he showed me a vision of Heaven; he and his family members were in a large boat on the ocean and he was gesturing for to me to follow him. The sense I received was that he was with the people he loved, and they were all together again and just fine. It validated my belief that the spirit realm reunites those from whom we've been separated by death and those whom we have helped enlighten and have cared for. From one lifetime to the next, we might change genders or even relationship roles, but we are always connected to our soul family. This is the reason some people might experience gender confusion today—because they are connected to memories of who they were in past lives. But if you are not hurting yourself or anyone else and not creating a space of separation, then it is good to honor your soul. In fact, it is right and just.

In thinking about my father's death, I know that it is our birthright to feel, sense, smell, and hear spirit through our God-given senses to help us navigate this lifetime. This is why our loved ones in the spirit realm send us healing messages that we can comprehend. Not to mention, when spirit decides to pay us a visit and when they feel we're ready for healing during our mourning process, our loved ones will do everything in their power to bring us comfort in our grief. They want to show us that even though they may have lost their body (shell), they are continually here in spirit, watching over us. In fact, they are so eager to let us know they are still part of our lives, but they don't want to scare us in the process—which is why many of these visitations are more subtle than overt.

When your heart is open enough to receive the blessings and the messages, you will most likely experience unexpected synchronicities, prophetic dreams, and/or symbolic occurrences—whatever transmission is easiest for them and you. When this happens, it's important to immediately stop and reflect on the visitations and the messages you have been given—most of all, trust the messages and live by them. Better yet, journal about them! Don't forget to date them for later reference. If these occurrences happen to two or more of your loved ones, don't be a doubting Thomas. Pay close attention!

Paying attention can be a difficult life lesson (one I'm still learning, as I can still fall into a pattern of doubt); simply opening your heart space and allowing confirmation to follow from the spirit world has made me stronger in my faith and my unconditional trust in spirit.

I am frequently asked, "Why don't I ever get spirit visitations from my dead loved ones?" Often, it may mean you are not aligned in mind, body, and soul. It all comes down to calming your own energy, especially if you are in the midst of mourning. If you dedicate yourself to prayer and meditation, and if you learn to balance and ground your chakras (energy centers), this will lead to deep healing—which will strengthen your connection to the spirit world. Just ask!

If you wish to educate yourself on this subject, seek a spiritual energy healing mentor—or better yet, book healing sessions for yourself periodically. This will bring joy, clarity, and vitality to your life and well-being. It will also help you return to your soul purpose and your connection to a much greater source. It will enable you to honor your inner calling.

If you are ready to receive Divine universal messages yourself, learn to ask with clarity to see specific signs either before bed or before you start your day. I know now that our loved ones want to help us, but they require our permission. Once you build up your confidence, simply trust and set fear to the side. Don't forget to acknowledge your loved ones by offering some sort of gesture followed by a smile and a warm virtual hug from your heart space. Give thanks for the connection.

Everything has an eternal identity, even though matter is transient. Too often, we struggle to comprehend that God our Divine creator offers many dimensions of existence in the celestial kingdom. The magnitude of the mysteries of the universe is greater than anything we can know.

Trust that the more you are aware of the messages you are given by spirit, the more time your loved ones who have passed over will spend with you. Be patient and persistent. Keep in mind that you are not pestering them in any way. When a spirit crosses over, just as my father's did, it leaves its earthly worries and ailments behind. Your loved one is able to heal and reflect on their human experience, which will lead them to their next mission. It is wise to help them celebrate their soul.

At the same time, spirit wants us to remember the good old days, not the time leading up our loved ones' passing. Although I mourned my father's death for a long time, I came to see that for many, the soul leaves the body before the time of actual death. Especially for those who slip into a coma, there is a chance that the soul might be bargaining with God to receive a second shot at life. They might be given an instruction by spirit to "spread the good news." In some cases, our soul can prepare us through our intuition for the actual time that we will depart our body. (This is true for many saints, sages, and spiritual teachers who predicted their actual deaths years in advance.).

Allow this awareness to only bring comfort that there is no such thing as death of our soul but death of the body we once borrowed. The transition phase after a loved one's death is a good time to say the words, "It's OK to go back home now." Essentially, we are all walking each other back home. Naturally, we mourn our loved ones because of our sadness, but those in the spirit realm are freer than ever, no longer mourning the lives they once lived. They are happy and at peace...and they want you to be, too.

CHAPTER 6

The Year I Surrendered to My Intuition

—————————————

"By awakening the Native American teachings, you come to
the realization that the earth is not something simply that you
build upon and walk upon and drive upon and take for granted.
It is a living entity. It has consciousness."—Edgar Cayce

"For the eyes of the LORD move to and fro throughout
the earth that he may strongly support those whose
HEART is completely HIS." —*2 Chronicles 16:9*

My life transformed when I moved to Calgary with my two daughters in the wake of leaving Vinny. This is when I met the man who would become my husband. After marrying, we bought a house in 2008 and I gave birth to my third daughter, Jessica. Luckily, the distance between me and Vinny helped us to cultivate a strong friendship. After all, we had two daughters together, created in love, and I expected Vinny to be there for them. But I had moved on, and my path was clearly transforming.

Things yet again took a dramatic turn near the end of 2014. Between September and December, we endured three deaths in the family. My brother Tim, my uncle Leonard, and my stepfather Christian all passed away. This took an enormous toll on my mother, who now lived nearly four hours away. I was the youngest of six siblings, but I was also the one that my mother leaned on most heavily in her times of need. I spread myself thin for others but rarely received this kindness in return. In a time of need, I usually found comfort from going within. I often paid for my mother's bus fare from Edmonton to Calgary, and although I attempted to convince her to move closer to me so that she wasn't so alone, she always ended up refusing. It was intensely stressful, because although she depended on me, she was never willing to meet me halfway and make the relationship easier on me.

My mother had had a hard life, it's true...but there was a sense of resentment she seemed to carry toward me that was hard to understand. It was almost as if she felt that I owed her my life, so she had no qualms about taking advantage of my kindness. And there was seldom any gratitude or reciprocity connected to that expectation. It was a relationship of tough love that was quite hurtful to endure. Despite the fact that I bent over backwards for her and didn't really want anything from her, it never felt like it was enough. I learned to offer forgiveness and abide by my daughterly duties, but only after setting up healthy, energetically protective boundaries. She would always be my mom and I would always be her daughter, but it was easiest to love her from a distance.

While the deaths of three loved ones were obviously difficult for my mother, they also impacted me in strange ways. After each death, I kept getting diagnosed with strep throat. This was mysterious to me, because I was healthy and active in my life, and I didn't understand why my illness was recurring. Between the funeral arrangements, long-distance driving, and all the antibiotics I had to take, my body and spirit felt like they were beginning to weaken.

Thankfully, throughout these deaths, my brother Greg was there for me and was even able to incorporate native practices into Tim's funeral, which I appreciated. All the same, it was hard to accept that my other siblings were not stepping up to help my mother at this time. It was incredibly draining, and I knew I couldn't do it on my own. My sister Claudia, who was raised by my grandmother, came to Tim's funeral, but she refused to contribute or play a significant role. Because I felt so disrespected, I refused to waste my energy on her and chose to keep a healthy distance throughout the funeral, as I do today—offering forgiveness and compassion from afar.

Once the funerals were over and the time for mourning kicked in, I allowed myself to reflect on all that had happened. Trying to keep my composure around my mourning mother and being the shoulder to cry on placed me in a position I hadn't been in since the loss of my father 12 years before.

As sick as I was, in the comfort of my own home, an incredible force came over me. I felt like I had literally hit rock bottom, and I simply couldn't go on like this. I was sick, tired, drained, and exhausted by the need to be strong for others in my life. Unlike the years of living with Vinny's family, who were incredibly supportive and kind to me, I was in a place in my life where I was the one taking care of my family, with almost no help from other family members. Alone in my bedroom, I collapsed to my knees, my face against the floor. I pleaded to the Divine for forgiveness, and I repetitively asked, "What is it you want from me? I give up doing everything on my own. Please show me what you want from me? Lead me! I surrender!"

Religion had never played a huge role in my life up until this point. I grew up not going to church, and although my Filipino husband's family was devoutly

Catholic, we rarely saw them and didn't really partake in the religious holidays aside from a few. But for whatever reason, I felt as though there were a greater calling for me and I simply needed to surrender to it. I could no longer attempt to exert control over my life. Something in me that was much bigger than my ego had taken over.

At that moment, another force nudged me as I glanced at a student Bible on my nightstand that had been gifted to me by a co-worker after my father's death; this book never seemed to leave my side.

Behind the front cover was written: "May 24, 2002. Dear Cindy, it's a privilege to share with you the love of Jesus. My prayer for you is that you grow to know him personally, and there's no better way to do that than by reading His word, the Bible. This book you hold in your hands is power, and it's life. May the peace of God fill your heart and bless you and your household. With Love, Edith"

I had briefly glanced at it when it was given to me, but seldom opened it. Now, in my time of need, it felt like an important symbol, especially considering that a mysterious stranger had gifted my mother a Bible randomly during an especially dark moment in her life before I was born—and had later vanished into thin air, to my mother's surprise. Could he have been temporarily Heaven-sent on a mission to save her soul?

I decided to pick up the book and open it at random. Before opening it, I asked the question, "What do you want to show me?" followed by "What do I need to do next?" I was convinced that spirit would give me a sign. Allowing my fingers to flow, I opened the book up to *John 3:5*: "Jesus answered, most assuredly, I say to you, unless one is born of water and the spirit, he cannot enter the kingdom of God."

Reading this immediately made me wonder if I had even been baptized as an infant. Wiping my tear-stained face, I called my mother. Unsurprisingly, she informed me that I had not been baptized. Although my mother had her own personal connection to God, she still maintained a great deal of bitterness toward the Catholic church. She'd absorbed the doctrine but rejected the church as an institution.

When it became clear that I wanted to get baptized and called my mother to discuss it, she was upset. "No, you shouldn't tie yourself to the church that way!" she insisted. But I was beyond listening to her, especially with respect to something as important as this, so I quickly hung up.

I followed my instincts and fasted and prayed for an entire week, eliminating meat from my diet and increasing my vegetable intake. Being a rare O negative blood type, it was very challenging for me, but I intuitively knew that this was what I needed. This loss pretty much altered the way I thought of life, and it motivated me with an intense desire to help make a difference in the world. I was led to research the true meaning of life and death, and the distinction between spirituality and religion.

Within days, I signed up with the nearest Catholic parish and inquired about getting baptized. I was assigned to a one-year program of Biblical study and masses,which was required for any adult seeking baptism. This opened up my life in a brand-new way, and I immediately began to experience the presence of Jesus and the Holy Spirit. Surprisingly, spiritual gifts started presenting themselves to me. It was as though my third eye had quickly opened without any effort. I'd reached a turning point of purpose and opened a door on spirit that I never closed after that.

For me, baptism felt like an important gesture because it was a way of shedding karma. I knew that after all I'd been through, I wanted purification. I wanted to lift the negative energy that surrounded me, and to feel more connected to God and His universe. Prior to this, I had lived more in my body than in my spirit, so this new decision to fully commit to God felt like it was ordained by a higher power.

Baptism was also full surrender to Christ. And I longed more than anything to empty the contents of my "self," and release my ego, which I'd struggled with for far too long. I knew that the ego was a protective mechanism that I'd fallen back on, but that it ultimately had the power to harm me if I let it run amok and was unaware of my Divine journey.

In the months leading up to my baptism, I felt almost as if I were Jesus walking the earth. My dreams were filled with God, Jesus, celestial beings, visions of guidance and warnings for myself and others (which were later confirmed), visitations from the spirits of passed loved ones obligated to help heal others through the laying of hands, and images of aspects from my waking life that needed to be healed—from infertility to emotional chaos.

One day, in a dream, a portrait of Jesus that I had in my house came to life. The prince of peace appeared before my eyes in vivid detail. His deep, blue-green eyes glistened like sunlight reflected on the ocean. A feeling of peace, purity, and reverence came over me. I felt like I finally understood all that is. Similar to my dreams of my father, no words were exchanged, but the information came through telepathically. As I sank deep into His eyes (the seat of his soul), Jesus informed me that He has and have had many lives, and we must find time to seek Him from within daily, even if only through a thought or gesture. He seemed to be saying that He deserved humans' attention and respect, and invited us to lean on Him more than ever before...because He loved us more than we could possibly know.

The entire experience was quite brief, but it was extremely sacred and heartfelt. When I woke up at 5:55 a.m. (prophetic dreams are said to come between 3 and 6 a.m.), I had the strong sense of smelling a home-cooked meal. The first word that came to me was "feast." The smell was so intense that I shook my head to stir myself awake. Had I left the slow cooker on overnight? I fell out of bed and stumbled to the kitchen, but there was nothing on the stove or elsewhere. The delightful aroma lingered with me throughout the day, no matter where I went. I asked others if they could smell it, but they didn't. It was an experience I will never forget—a natural, Divine connection without a physical source, straight from Jesus in spirit Himself.

As with every spiritual experience, I looked into this one more to try to make sense of it, reflecting. It was April so I realized we were also in the time of Passover, which Jews celebrate to commemorate their liberation by God from slavery in ancient Egypt, and their freedom as a nation under the leadership of Moses. I wondered if the dream and the smell of the feast were a personal invitation to the Passover feast that would be Christ's last supper. I found the idea extremely comforting, because it made me very much aware that we are never alone. And the dream itself was a personal parable that I could choose to embody so that I, too, would radiate love and peace to others.

Over time, I came to understand that anyone can receive prophetic dreams, which might include messages of love and blessing, premonitions, guidance, and even warnings about lower vibrations in our midst. If I had a question, I realized that I could simply ask for an answer in a dream before falling asleep with these specific intentions, and that any answer I received would be Divinely guided—if not in a dream state, a meditative on. Whatever the case, I would make a point to listen for it through signage, songs on the radio, or people who crossed my path that resonated with me. It always felt like confirmation that I was on the path right, in the right place at the right time. I knew that the more I responded to my dream interpretations and spiritual nudges, the more I showed spirit that I could trust in what was being shared and the stronger my faith would be.

Angelic forms also began coming to me even more frequently...but strangely, leading up to my baptism, I felt a sense of tension, as well as wild energies of spiritual warfare, around me. When I stood still, as if I were observing from a bird's eye view, it was as though I were walking the temptations of the 40 days and 40 nights that Jesus once had. People were talking about death around me, I was experiencing the tension of other people's road rage, and my daughter Jade's vehicle was totalled by an accident when someone collided into her. It was if these lower energies were trying to get to me before my baptism. And unfortunately, many people simply were not supportive of my awakening.

The evening before my baptism ceremony, out of nowhere, I was at my church when my godmother pulled me to the side and asked me about the dreams I'd been having, which I spoke open about at our congregation. "Cindy, you have to rebuke them," she said. "These could be signs from the devil, to tempt you."

I was rattled by her assertion, especially since I'd felt nothing but pure love and compassion from the visions I'd had. After a year, I didn't understand why she was attacking me all of a sudden, when I'd clearly experienced spiritual blessings and sightings of God and His living spirits. But she continued to insist that I had to reject the dreams...which took me back to the ways that my mother had rejected the many supernatural events in her life out of nothing but fear.

I shook my head vehemently and disagreed with my godmother. To me, it felt like a slap in the Divine's face. Confused and disappointed, I went back to join the circle that had gathered, and people could see that I was disturbed and had been crying. An assistant of one of the deacons later approached me in private to ask if I was OK. I told her about what had happened. She sat and listened to me, then said, "Everyone has their own relationship with God. Some people see the purity of the kinds of visions you've been having, and others don't. You can't let her get to you."

The deacon came over afterwards and also attempted to reassure me. "Cindy, around the time of baptism, it's normal to experience a lot of tension. Deaths tend to happen, too. Souls who are confused might let these lower energies get to them, but it's a test that you are strong enough to face. With your God sightings you've shared throughout the year, you are very blessed.'

He held both his hands over me in prayer as a way of blessing and said, "Thank you, Father, for blessing your gifts through Cindy, and I pray that you will continue to lead her in your presence and to do great works." This brought me back to the healing I'd received from the three elders, who'd also prayed over me the same way when I was seven years old. I began to realize that the prayer of intention doesn't have to be from a priest, after all (although they mean well).

I felt peace come over me once more. I knew that my relationship to the Divine was strong, authentic, and grounded in love rather than fear. My visions were proof that I was connected to something that exceeded what the church could provide. I could feel the pull on my heartstrings for a deeper connection, a broader mission. I didn't feel superior because of this; rather, I felt that it was my duty to share my stories with the other church-goers so that they, too, could experience peace and reassurance with their experiences, especially if they were unsure of whether they were within God's spiritual laws. It felt like God's way of asking me to "spread the good news" with humility, to bring hope and awareness of His goodwill to all.

So I continued to let go and shed the trappings of my ego and fear, as I knew that surrender was the engine that would drive my transformation and lead me to my Divine purpose.

On our pathway to enlightenment, we will be called again and again to surrender more of ourselves. If we keep allowing our fear-based desires, attractions, repulsions, and limitations to seep in so that we are not in alignment with our soul growth, we will continue to be estranged from our Divine loving energy source: God, our creator.

Many of us will face tests in our lives, and we will eventually have no other choice but to keep surrendering until we become awakened and aligned in our minds, bodies, and souls. God and His universe want to help us achieve our soul's desires in this lifetime, but so often, fear becomes a hindrance that blocks us from the light. But fear is a liar, an illusion.

We must learn to heed the spiritual nudges, especially in the midst of rock-bottom moments...which is when grace is always available to us if we allow ourselves to turn to the light, where we are always safe.

CHAPTER 7

When a Surge of Spirit Hits, We All Get Wet!

"Watch your thoughts; they become words
Watch your words; they become actions
Watch your actions; they become habits
Watch your habits; they become character
Watch your character; it becomes your destiny."
—Lao Tzu

"Herein is our love made perfect, that we may of judgement: because
AS HE IS, SO ARE WE IN THIS WORLD." —*1 John 4:17*

A year after attending masses, I was ready for my baptismal process, which my family and I attended. At this point, all of my daughters had already been baptized. Two years after she was born, my youngest daughter Jessica was baptized at my in-laws' behest, and I also included Jade in that process. Jasmine was living on her own at this time, but she and I had always experienced a deep spiritual connection and were baptized at around the same time at different churches.

The last year had revealed so much to me about what I felt my vision in life was: to be a warrior of pure love, peace, and light on behalf of God. The prophecies I'd received in dreams and visions, as well as the visitations from spirit, had filled me with deep reverence and humility. I finally had the sense that I knew my purpose. Yes, I'd been "dropped" into this world unexpectedly at a young age, but my sense of connection to God had finally given me a home spiritually, alleviating that sense of homesickness I'd always had. I had always known that we were were puppets controlled by an invisible Divine thread— that we were here on a short mission in the body we'd chosen to inhabit.

We were running a little late to church when we spotted a Chinese woman who was also part of the baptismal program. Her name was also Cindy. She sat in the third pew from the front altar. Although there was a packed house, oddly enough, there were three available spots—which my husband, my daughter Jessica, and I hurriedly took. Cindy turned and smiled at me. She'd placed her purse and belongings between our seats, and she was approximately an arm's length away.

During the mass, I felt the urge to simply attune to the presence of God and zone out from the background noise of feet shuffling and kids fidgeting so I could paint a vivid picture of the Gospel in my mind that day. I instantly bowed my head and closed my eyes. Suddenly, I felt a strong breeze on my right, which literally *whooshed* the sides of my long bangs forward. Although I acknowledged it mentally, I kept my eyes closed, dismissing the movement and chalking it up to a small child playing behind us.

As the reader ended the passage he was reading, the baptismal group was called up to the altar. The group comprised me and the other Cindy, and we were led by our group leader to the back of the stage and to the back boardroom, as we reflected on what had been shared on stage during mass.

As soon as the three of us entered the room, out of nowhere, Cindy tugged urgently at my sleeve and began talking to me in broken English. Although it took me several moments to figure out what she was trying to communicate, it was clear that it was important. Her expression was a mixture of excitement and confusion.

"Cindy...Cindy?" she said, almost in disbelief.

I attempted to remain calm. "Yes, what's the matter?"

"You know when we were sitting back there?" She pointed back out to the pew in front of the stage through the walls that now surrounded us.

"Yes?" I had a gut feeling that she, too, would comment on the strong breeze that had come out of nowhere.

"Well, when the pastor was talking, my mind was thinking bad thoughts. I was thinking about how my coworker is so mean, and how much I hate her!" I frowned slightly, trying not to be too judgmental. "Oh no, Cindy! During mass? OK…" I waited patiently for her to continue.

She nodded, guilt coming over her face. "As I was thinking bad thoughts, Cindy, I felt a strong tap on my left upper arm. I stopped and turned, and then I looked at you. Cindy, you had your head down, your eyes were closed, and both your hands were upon your lap. I didn't even see you move!"

In reflecting, I recognized that she had probably felt the tap just at the same time I'd felt the breeze.

Our group leader listened in silence.

I was trying to make sense of what Cindy was telling me, although I felt it was quite normal in my world at this point in time. Who had tapped her? It certainly hadn't been me. And was that person or being the same one that had generated the breeze I'd felt so strongly?

"After that tap, I didn't think bad again. Thank you, thank you, Cindy!" she gushed gratefully.

I smiled but didn't feel comfortable taking credit for something I hadn't done, although I was glad that her looking at me had given her a sense of calm. "Please, don't thank me. It was God's way of reminding you not to fall prey to negative thinking at church, or at all, for that matter."

Intuitively, I felt that perhaps the tap Cindy felt had been from my dad, because the following day, I was woken up to a tap on my left shoulder while I was lying in bed as both my daughter and husband were still snoring into my left ear. I knew by now that a part of mediumship was literally feeling the presence of spirit. Besides, it seemed like something my father would have done in church, especially if he'd known that he was interrupting her negative thinking.

I didn't tell Cindy any of this. I didn't want to overwhelm her, but I knew she needed to experience what she had. It was extra confirmation that God was real. She needed to experience God as tangible and remember that His spirit is fully alive—not something locked in a doctrine or a set of rules. I knew that the signs would come to us when we were ready for them. And they weren't there as threats, but as wakeup calls affirming that there is so much more to life than most of us imagine...and that someone is always watching over us.

A couple weeks after my encounter with Cindy in our parish, she informed me that, out of the blue, the coworker she'd once had issues with had become her best friend. It was one of the early moments of feeling that I was an intercessor, someone who had the capacity to pray or appeal to God on another person's behalf.

I now know from experience that when I pray for someone, or when I am involved in any kind of healing work for them, I help ignite God/Jesus/Holy Spirit/the universe and bring them to the person. At that point, I am content in my awareness that I did my part...and now it's the free will of the other person to walk toward God, honoring their soul by being fully open to receiving His Divine guidance.

I try to help people remember that the spirit world is always here to support us in our daily lives for the greater good. Ask and you shall receive! It doesn't matter where you're at, what you have or have not done, or where your belief system lies. Assistance from spirit should be sacredly honored with respect for what exists beyond the veil; it should inspire you to turn toward what is being shown to you, and to share it with those around you. It should motivate you to spread good news among your neighbors to give them hope and awareness of the blessings and compassionate heart of the Divine.

I barely knew Cindy, other than she was new to Canada and had a son around the same age as my daughter, Jessica. Did it matter? No, not at all. This single encounter brought us closer in our relationship until the end of our baptism program. That mysterious experience in church felt like a necessary one for both of us. It had opened both our eyes to the depth of God's love for each and every one of us. For me, it reaffirmed my awareness of our Divine connections with our guardian angels. Passed loved ones and their vital messages come to us right from the energy source: our creator, who blesses us with downloads of unconditional love and compassion. Truly, there is no disconnection among humans, spirit, and Mother Earth. God's blessings are in everything.

This is why we must strive to create peace and harmony for our soul and live a life of greatness and kindness, with discipline and a self-nurturing belief in ourselves. Although I didn't share my desires for Cindy with her, I wanted her to bring this awareness to her everyday living. It is crucial for all of us to forego time wasted on negative thinking and make the most of our time here by living with a soul purpose that supports God's wishes for us.

With every supernatural experience, we should not question or judge, but rather, take the lesson to heart, trust in it, be of service, and demonstrate through our own experiences that we are committed to helping others in their journeys. We need not boast or take credit for anyone else's transformation; rather, we should spread goodness as we share and bear witness to His full blessings. He fully appreciates the acknowledgment, respect, and personal connection. I believe that all sacred prophets who practice and teach mindfulness, compassion, unconditional love, and attachment to nothing yet connection to everything have been touched by God's healing energies.

I knew on that day that if I could bring any news to my brothers and sisters to strengthen their faith, as well as bring hope and happiness to their souls, I was exactly where I needed to be.

CHAPTER 8

Your Spiritual Gifts Are Universal Blessings

"I believe that the only true religion consists of
having a good heart." —Dalai Lama

"Truly I tell you, whatever you did for one of the least of these
brothers and sisters of mine, you did for me." —*Matthew 25:40*

I found myself surrendering to God's gifts even more deeply. There was no way to run from it. Since surrendering to God essentially meant surrendering to His universe, I discovered a magical sense of connection to everything around me. It felt as if the heaviness of being stuck in human flesh, form, and ego was automatically lifted and replaced with a Divine light and larger-than-life strength I'd never truly known. It seemed to me that everywhere I looked, I received immediate universal signs of mystical love and illuminating light that instantly took over every cell of my body, as well as everything and everyone around me—leaving the physical me in the passenger seat, for the most part.

I had surrendered to my intuition without truly knowing what that even meant or entailed. But I knew that God was sending me a clear message: "It's time for you to be awakened and to be of service, in my name." Previously, I'd

52

felt a vaguer connection to God, and most of my life had consisted of living in the moment and taking care of my day-to-day business. But I'd still been floating through life without a deeper sense of purpose. Now, I was finally taking ownership of my path and agreeing to accept what had been given to me. I was willing to trust in this unknown process of surrender and awakening, all for my highest good.

During this time, I was granted intense downloads of flashbacks of childhood memories, which came across my consciousness like Polaroid images: my loneliness and alienation from other people as a young child, the way asthma had limited my life, dealing with my mother's alcoholic rampages, and scrounging around for food in an almost-bare kitchen. It all became clear to me: Love entails suffering. I was able to look back on those moments and make the connection between my early childhood suffering and being healed on the spot through the laying of hands at the age of seven. I recognized so many years later that in the moment of healing, God had been personally speaking to me. He had said, "I'll heal you now, and when you are older and ready for me, you will be of service."

My spiritual awakening didn't change my home life much. My husband had already been baptized as a baby and attended church once in a while. As a family, whether we went to church or not, we all accepted and believed in a higher power, which was present in our daily habits. Ever since they were little, I had encouraged my children to be grateful for everything that came to them. I didn't always do it explicitly, but I made sure that my language and my behavior reflected that sense of gratitude for life's blessings. Every single one of my daughters grew up with that attitude, so although they took slightly different spiritual paths as they came of age, they were always entrenched in some form of faith and reverence for life's blessings.

But for me, my spiritual journey took on a greater sense of urgency after that moment of awakening, when I pleaded to the universe to show me how I could be of service to humanity. After I decided to get baptized, prophetic dreams came to me with full force. I knew that what I was experiencing was holy, a deeper sacred calling that words couldn't do justice to. All of it was simply beyond my capacity to make up. My husband was supportive, but given that he was so analytical, he always attempted to make sense of what I was experiencing.

"You can't try to make sense of something that's beyond logic!" I'd laugh, trying not to take it too seriously. But at other times, I was frustrated. I wanted so badly to open his eyes so he could see and feel what I was seeing and feeling. But here, too, was another place where I needed to surrender. I knew that he was on his own spiritual path, as we all are. Every single one of us is energetically vibrating at our own unique level. I wondered if I had been placed on his path to be a living example of what God truly is in spirit.

In the meantime, the deeper I surrendered, the more I felt the universe opening up to me in peculiar ways. God and His universe will reveal more as we continue to ascend.

On Saturday, March 3, 2016, a vivid dream vision came to me. In it, I saw a married couple whom I did not know personally. However, I was quite aware that they volunteered a lot at the parish I attended. We periodically bumped into each other, and I genuinely liked them. They were kind and pious people, always so accommodating and ready to make me and others who came through feel welcomed.

In my vision, the husband was laboring at a distance; he seemed to be putting something together, while the wife appeared to be assisting. As I was taking in what was being presented to me, Jesus's overwhelming presence came in above them to the right. A brilliant white, warm, loving, and peaceful glow radiated over the couple. I could feel Jesus telling me telepathically that He wanted me to deliver them a message. It was hard for me to interpret, because Jesus was expressing Himself in verses that were challenging to translate into feelings and words of healing. He went on to share that He acknowledged all their help in giving back to humanity, and that they should never worry about money or materialistic, earthly things; as long as they continued to serve Him, He would always provide. His communication was ultimately brief and straight to the point.

As soon as I understood the download and that He was finished, I felt him shoot an instant energetic surge of unconditional love straight into my heart. It felt like a thick cord connecting His heart to mine. The love infused my entire body, and it felt so strong that I woke up grabbing at my heart, tears of love and compassion flowing from my eyes.

I had read before that prophetic dreams come between the hours of 3 and 6 a.m., and consecutive numbers are significant. I glanced at my alarm clock, which informed me that it was 3:33 a.m., a time I was already begin to link to Jesus appearing to me when I needed Him most.

Half asleep, I grabbed my cell phone, remembering that I just might have an email at hand for the couple I'd dreamed about. Rummaging through my group emails, I found it and quickly sent them an email relaying the message that Jesus had had for them. I crossed my fingers in the hope that it would be well received and would make perfect sense to them.

The following day was our usual Sunday mass gathering. I spotted the wife, whom I'd seen in my dream. I was eager to talk to her, but I decided to wait until mass was over to see if she would confirm the veracity of the email I'd sent early yesterday morning. Once mass was over, I hastened over to her and pulled her aside.

"Did you receive my email early Saturday morning?" I asked. "I dreamed about you and your husband!"

"What email? You actually dreamed about us?" I could practically see her melting right then and there. Like many others in our parish, she knew I was a prophetic dreamer. She grabbed my hand and sat us both down. "Please tell me—what was your dream about?"

I closed my eyes, attempting to recall every word of the message I'd sent, which she'd apparently not received. I didn't want to leave anything out. As I finished relaying to her all that I'd seen and felt, I could hear her sniffling. I opened my eyes, caught off guard as she wiped her tears away.

"Did I say something wrong?" I asked, confused.

She lightly slapped my leg. "Cindy, you are gifted with the prophecy of Jesus! There's no way you could have known otherwise!"

I was genuinely surprised. "What do you mean?"

"My husband and I spent hours on Friday volunteering and feeding the homeless. Then we stayed up until almost past midnight putting together pack-ages for the homeless. That's what your dream visit revealed!"

"Get out of here!" I myself was shocked. "I guess Jesus is acknowledging you both for doing a good deed for humanity."

She smiled at me. "Praise God!" We hugged, and she went off to share this holy message with her husband.

It was a beautiful reminder that, in many cases, there are a lot of kind-hearted people out in the world giving back, sacrificing themselves to be of service and sometimes wondering if they are doing the right thing. Often, they don't receive the gratitude or acknowledgement they deserve, or if they do, maybe not as often as they should. After my sacred dream visit, I was touched that this respectful working couple had always remained humble as they gave back to humanity. And in the process, they were creating a continual stream of positive karma.

The dream also showed me the importance of selfless service. If you are someone who loves to give back and to be of service, understand that God our creator sees all that you have chosen to do with your free will—and He acknowledges and appreciates you when you honor His lead. Be affirmed that the universe will carry you through even if you are not aware of its support in the present moment.

The universe always has our backs and is always orchestrating on our behalf, behind the scenes, which we cannot fully understand or see in the here and now. Everything is in Divine order, and is meant to be. This is where our strength and faith come into play. I felt fortunate to be delivering a message from the Divine to these beautiful people, whom I considered true earth angels.

CHAPTER 9

The Bliss of Meditation

"Do not run away. Run INWARD." —Rumi

"There is a way that seems right to a man, but its
end is the way of death." —*Proverbs 14:12*

As the months went by and I received communion, I began to recognize a trend during my visits to church and my interactions with the people around me. I saw plenty of people praying, but I wasn't always convinced that this enhanced their relationship to spirit. After all, while prayer is wonderful, it isn't enough—you also need space to actually listen for the answers.

Adding meditation to my prayer regimen came easily to me when I created time daily. I personally found that it was a faster entrance into spirit. In a spiritual class I once took, somebody mentioned the power of cultivating a practice of "morning pages," where you wake up first thing in the morning and write in stream-of-consciousness style without censoring any of the content that comes out. When you dedicate yourself to this practice, it's remarkable what comes out of it. It becomes a space for intuitive insight and messages from God. And it's a lot like attending church—you respect the time you've set.

Just as morning pages are a meditation, there are many ways to meditate. Typically, I pray for myself and others, and express my gratitude for all that I've been given. Then, I ask a question I feel stuck on and that I want answers for before allowing myself to simply slip into a silent, meditative state. During my meditation, I usually get the insight I desire, as I've cleared my mind and gone into this space with a clear intention. My mind and heart are open, and I give myself over to God. Sometimes the answers will come in the form of visions, or as simple messages. If I don't receive any answers during my meditation, they'll inevitably come through dreams or other synchronicities, or sometimes both. Whatever the case, upon ending my meditation, I thank my Divine team that came forward to give me the message and ask them to help me throughout the day. Through the power of meditation, the gateways to the spiritual realm open and the universal signs come in to offer me confirmation of what I know or the answers that I need.

Meditation is about being in this constant dialogue with God. All too often, people pray without ensuring that they are open to God's response. Meditation offers that alignment, as it is a partnership with the Divine that is based on honoring and respecting the answers that flow in, and taking action on them.

Through meditation, I learned to heed my soul contract so that I always know what I am here to do. Being on this earth is not simply about calling on God when I need something; it is about making that deep connection in times of both perceived "bad" and perceived "good." Sometimes, the moments of difficulty are my greatest teacher; when something bad occurs, I can ask why it showed up on my path. With the answers I receive, I understand that it's possible for me to walk a different path—and I am always grateful for the lessons.

While meditation was not necessarily a part of the church's teachings, after I was baptized, the spiritual doors that opened led me to teachers beyond the church. I understood that it was up to me to climb over the wall of religion and find the deeper spiritual meaning in my life. While I had been called to the church, I understood that it didn't really matter which god anybody praised, as their devotion all led back to the same source. Because Jesus appeared to me repeatedly, and I could sense His loving surrender on the cross (almost as if I'd been there to witness his death and resurrection in a past life), my connection to Christianity was deep and immediate. But I didn't want it to be a barrier to my awareness of the New Age that I felt was upon us. Nothing would hinder my spiritual growth.

When I discovered Reiki, which I clearly saw as being connected to the Christian tradition of the laying of hands, I was immediately brought back to my childhood memory of being cured of my asthma. I vividly recalled the restoration of my lungs after the group of female elders lay their hands on me. After moving through my Reiki course, I could finally wrap my brain around the fact that every single one of us was a healer—and we can all heal one another. Later reflection through meditation led me to realize that being healed at such a young age was a message from God: "I will heal you now, and you will serve me when you are older."

Over time, I understood that a respect for spirit and all that lives beyond the veil was necessary. I was invited to move out of my comfort zone and to bring together prayer, meditation, morning pages, and energy healing.

During my daily quiet time with the Divine one day, an angelic image appeared in a brilliant light-filled setting. I was in a state of trance as I observed the image, which contained a rectangular box; inside the box were words in beautiful calligraphic writing: "Believe in love." Each word faded smoothly into the other, and after I received the message, it was replaced by a heart-shaped bubble that gradually grew until it absorbed the image altogether.

As I came back to consciousness, I looked outside my window...and there it was! The same angelic image with the heart-shaped cloud greeted me, as if to remind me of its proximity in my daily life. Just as I was about to grab my phone to take a photograph, I looked up and it immediately vanished into thin air.

Before I'd gone into my meditation, I had a simple question: "What universal message would you like to share?" Then, I simply let go of my consciousness, releasing everything around me. My sense of the message was that humankind has always played a crucial role in our world, and that it is time for a collective consciousness of peace and harmony to rise and take over our world, including our relationship to the earth and to ourselves and each other. Such is the power of love.

Meditation is the harbinger of a peace that enables us to limit our negative thoughts, reduce our stress, and live our purpose. I recommend beginning your day with 15 minutes minimum of meditation before you do anything else. If you have to wake up early, do so—but commit yourself to this practice. Then, take a pad of paper and a pen and write down everything that comes to mind: things you are grateful for, and things that are troubling your heart. Allow the prayer to come from your heart, and invite answers to a particular question you have. Then, take several minutes to simply breathe and be silent, and turn your prayer into a listening meditation. Although you might have a desired answer or response, it is vital to leave a space in your meditation for the abundance of Divine miracles to occur. God knows best.

Again, there are many forms of meditation, which I imagine as Divine connection to your intuitive right brain. You might choose to walk in nature, paint, sing, dance—whatever the case, do what you can to simply be in the stillness within. This is a beautiful way to fill your own cup with Divine energy. By finding your soul's connection to the Divine through your creativity, you will download healing directly from God. Honoring your creative self and allowing it to be a channel for Divine healing enables God's beauty to come through, so that when someone else encounters your work, they, too, experience that healing.

Meditation also helps us to recognize Divine love from within and to release the battles of ego from our minds. It helps us to eliminate the fear and chatter that disrupt our daily purpose in life. When we choose meditation, we not only learn how to ground, align, and balance our inner beauty—but we also attract this from our outer surroundings with all those whom we encounter. We alleviate the overwhelming circumstances in our lives and naturally welcome God's healing guidance.

Countless studies have revealed that meditation can make you smarter, happier, healthier, and also direct your inner spiritual compass to help you navigate life's ups and downs. Regular meditation can reduce stress, stimulate new brain cell formation, and even slow down the rate of brain cell aging!

If you're a newcomer to meditation, YouTube offers countless guided meditations in various durations so that you can gradually ease your way into longer periods of stillness. Binaural beats are especially beneficial; this kind of music has only been available through technology in the last hundred years, but the science behind it dates back millennia. The repetition of consistent, rhythmic sound has a variety of spiritual benefits, entraining our brain to experience states that take us out of the usual fight-or-flight response and into greater creativity, enhanced problem-solving, and more receptivity to the Divine. Pick a binaural beat that you can trust that resonates with you and makes it easier for you to go deep. All in all, with a good set of headphones and a phone, computer, or tablet connected to WiFi, you have a powerful healing tool at your disposal!

Remember to supplement your meditation with prayer, which is your direct channel of conversation to God and your Divine spiritual team, who help nourish and guide you through your journey. You can express gratitude for all that is in your life and mention your desires, while also acknowledging that you are open to receiving something greater that is aligned with your soul purpose. Be specific with your questions and intentions. To deepen into your meditative state, whether you are using a guided meditation or simply sitting in silence, settle into the energy of your breath—which will take you into a serene, soulful state.

I personally inhale Heaven (spirit) and exhale earth (flesh). Let yourself surrender and trust in the guidance of the Divine. Open your heart and listen in silence, for you'll find wisdom there. Be comfortable with the stillness that is deep within you, which will help you accept the Divine guidance as it flows in— perhaps in words, visions, or simple directives similar to what I shared above. You might choose to write down what came to you during meditation, but also know that the answers will continue to come throughout your day. Let yourself marinate in this holy state before you continue with your morning routine.

To better heighten your frequency of faith, love, and charity, try listening to and repeating positive guided affirmations (which you can also find on YouTube), possibly on your morning commute or during a workout regimen. It may take you a couple weeks to really settle into your meditative habit, especially if you are accustomed to running around and fulfilling other people's needs, but simply making a heartfelt effort to get back on track will help you. Over time, you'll also recognize how much better you feel when you honor your practice. As a mother, wife, daughter, niece, sister-in-law, grandmother, granddaughter, aunt, friend, entrepreneur, and author, I have found that my meditative space is a welcome refuge that helps me move back into my life's responsibilities with ease and clarity. I have discovered that balance is key, and I must fulfill my needs first by maintaining my health, happiness, and connection to God in whatever ways I can.

May we all be consciously aware as we create an environment of peace and harmony by *believing in love* in all that we say or do.

CHAPTER 10

Parables of Love

"Become the proof that God exists." —Mooji

"There is no fear in love. But perfect love out fear,
because fear had to do with punishment. The one who
fears is not made perfect in love." —*1 John 4:18*

While many of the gifts of my spiritual awakening became evident in the years following my baptism, I also experienced the darker side of connecting with healing energy. I discovered that there are many spiritual wolves in sheep's clothing...those who have the desire to peer beyond the veil, but in the service of controlling others and depleting them of their spiritual energy. In the day-to-day world, we are accustomed to witnessing the power plays that lead certain groups and individuals to oppress others. Sadly, the same is true in the spirit realm, and among those who are attuned to the power of the Divine.

In 2014, I was guided to seek out spiritual mentors and teachers. I did a great deal of my research online, which is how I found Jennifer and Don, who both taught classes in the area where I lived. From their testimonials and reputations, it was clear to me that they were Divinely gifted. So I went to their classes to see if their work resonated with me, and if I could learn from them.

Jennifer was the first teacher I met in person. She taught classes in angel communication in Calgary. I brought my daughter Jade along with me during the first class, and she was clearly bored by the content, but I was enthralled by Jennifer's connection to the angels. During the class, Jennifer received a clear picture from Archangel Michael that I would someday write a book...this was the first time anyone had ever suggested such a thing, so I was astonished. As Jennifer channeled the information, she relayed it to me—but there were so many details that it was overwhelming to track them all. After the class, I went up to Jennifer and asked for further details, but she simply smiled and said, "Sorry, but when I'm in a trance and connecting with the angels, I don't remember anything."

I figured that perhaps, although the information had come through so clearly, the details weren't mine to know at this time. However, I was intrigued by the idea of writing a book, because at the time, I was journaling a great deal about my visions and meditations. I kept a detailed record of all the supernatural events I had lived through...all my encounters with the unknown. It simply felt important that I do this. I couldn't help but wonder whether or not my observations would someday make it into a book.

I ended up taking a class with Jennifer on mediumship, and over time, she came to respect me for my own spiritual insights. At some point, she asked me to accompany her during her psychic readings—to be an apprentice of sorts. I immediately agreed—although I later came to regret my decision.

During her readings, I felt almost as if I were being energetically drained. An excruciating headache came over me, almost as if somebody was hammering at the back of my head. I didn't even consider that I had been psychically attacked. I simply went home and didn't think about it. But the headache persisted, which led me to contact my Reiki teacher.

"I have a bad headache," I texted her. "Any thoughts on what I should do?"

We exchanged a few more texts, and I told her I'd been assisting Jennifer as she conducted her readings. "Did you make sure to energetically protect yourself?" my teacher asked.

I told her that I hadn't even considered the possibility, since I trusted Jennifer's field. My Reiki teacher immediately gave me a distance healing that cleared my headache, but she warned me that from now on, I had to ensure that I was protecting and shielding my energy at all times.

The lesson I came to gradually learn was that Jennifer was not someone I could trust. Although I was drawn to her capacity to communicate with the angels, which I wholeheartedly believed, I came to learn that she was manipulating the energy to her benefit, which was a way of feeding her insecurities. And some of the things she said gave me pause.

Because I was a hairdresser, I sometimes worked on her hair. Jennifer often told me that she got shivers when I touched her. "You have so much healing energy, I just want to absorb it!" she said.

At the time, I thought this was simply a compliment, but I later came to recognize that it was a sign that she was an energy vampire; that is, in order to maintain her own energetic "high," she drained energy from others. And because of her spiritual facade, few people knew this.

During my journey, I continued to "shop around" for other spiritual teachers. That was when I met Ramona, a psychic medium who could also see people's past lives. Once, when I was sitting with her, she informed me, "You're the incarnation of Sir Lancelot, of King Arthur's Round Table! And I'm the person who was responsible for your beheading."

Ramona seemed genuinely shocked at this information, which had spontaneously come to her, and so was I. I barely knew who Lancelot was, but I began to do my own research. Once, when Jennifer came to me to get her hair done, I told her about Ramona's insight about my past life as Lancelot. Jennifer simply looked at me, her mouth wide open in amazement. "That's so strange!" She closed her eyes, and I could tell that she was accessing other realms in that moment. When she opened them, she gave me a strange look. "Now I know why you're so familiar. I know who you are. I know who we were."

"What are you talking about?" I asked.

"You were Lancelot, and I was the queen, Gwenevere, with whom you were having an affair. Ramona was the chambermaid who informed the king about your faithlessness and had you beheaded."

At that point, I knew that I had to detach from both Ramona and Jennifer, and to clear whatever karma I'd accumulated. I didn't harbor any resentment toward them—I simply understood that they were not the teachers I was look-ing for. Through my own energetic work, I cleared my attachments to them. I was no longer Sir Lancelot (or was I?). Either way, it was time to move on.

Months after my encounters with Jennifer, I met Don, who was a well-known shaman. When I went to one of his classes, he looked me straight in the eye and said, "Cindy, I knew you'd come. I manifested you." I could feel the power in his energy work, so I saw him every month for an en-tire year. I didn't know it at the time, but his manipulation of energy was more vampirism than clearing. After he worked on me, he'd assure me that the aches and pains I felt in my body were simply part of the process. Don also seemed to have an innate sense of my own capacity as a healer. One day, I told him about a powerful supernatural experience I'd recently had. I was at the grocery store and asked one of the workers for help in placing some empty apple boxes inside the trunk of my car. As I looked at the cart from which he was removing the boxes, I saw it physically disappear before my eyes! When he turned around to push the cart back to the store and saw that it was gone, he was totally bewildered. I wondered if perhaps the disappearance of the cart had to do with the fact that I felt bad asking for help, as the guy didn't look very happy in his position, let alone about assisting me. A couple days later, when I went back to the grocery store, I saw the same worker. He informed me that he'd found the cart at the front entrance of the store but was still confused, as he didn't know how someone could have taken it without our seeing it within seconds. Physically speaking, it was impossible.

Don smiled with a certain knowing as I told him my story. "You see what you can do with energy? You're powerful, Cindy. You have to take that power and do something with it."

Over the year that I worked with Don, I could feel aspects of my personality changing. I began buying more black clothes, particularly in the form of long capes, which was incredibly unusual, as my style was always light and cheerful. A good friend of mine advised me to cut ties with Don after I almost passed out at church one day. My heart felt closed, and I was gasping for air. It felt like I was incapable of receiving love.

Another woman I knew who was a healer told me of an alarming vision she'd had of Don during a session with him. She saw him taking on the form of a serpent and emerging from a pool of red water. She immediately felt uncomfortable and closed off her energy so that it was harder for him to work on her. I was there during the session, and it was clear that she wanted to let me know what was happening—but for some reason, she was blocked from doing so. When she told me about it over the phone later that day, she suggested that we consult with another healer—a powerful woman who could enter different dimensions to clear the effects of black magic. The impact of that healing was powerful. It felt as if a huge burden had been lifted from my heart, and I could finally see clearly, as I'd been moving through a fog for months.

Shortly afterwards, I messaged Don to end our sessions together. I didn't want to let him know that I understood how he was using his power, as I simply wanted to be done with him. So I made an excuse that I needed to save money... but it was obvious that he didn't believe me. He was in the process of building a healing lodge and needed my money, so he wanted to keep me on his good side so I would continue to help him. But I was tired of having my energies manipulated and my power drained. I recalled a story he'd told me about a woman he'd worked with who'd nearly died, and how others had blamed him. I recognized that from the very beginning, this had been a giant red flag.

During this time I was in the process of becoming Baptist, which enjoined me to be strong in my faith and allowed me to witness the strength of God yet again. I had a vivid dream in which I was attacked for withdrawing from Don. As I lay there in a REM state, I received a warning letting me know that Don was astral-traveling my way. Before I could call on Archangel Michael, it was too late. I could feel Don hovering over me as a black cloud, leaving me paralyzed from the wrists down.

Internally, all I could think was, *He got me, that bastard!* I attempted to release myself. Just then, a golden throne filled with a series of words that I later came to realize were from a Biblical passage, filled the space: "Peace I leave with you, my peace I give to you. Not as the world gives do I give to you." With that, th throne slammed into Don, who was pushed off of me, and I was surrounded by a radiant light of peace and love. I was able to awaken from that sleep and reflect. I automatically turned my emotions into love and left no room for fear. I sent Don prayers of forgiveness and healing to help bring peace into our respective journeys.

In retrospect, I recognize that Don and Jennifer were like fallen angels, lower energies trying to take energy from others in order to survive and cast their dark spells. Because I cut all ties, I simply wanted to move on. But a good friend who followed Don on Facebook later told me that his entire enterprise had collapsed after I detached from him.

Through a year-long process, I learned my lesson and now trusted in it. I knew that I needed to work out these karmic relationships and to better understand the spiritual warfare that was taking place at the hands of these so-called shaman healers. I now knew how important it was to educate ourselves about this spiritual warfare, and to coat ourselves with the armor of God. These days, I like to envision myself surrounded by a violet flame that only love can enter.

In thinking about the spiritual attack in the dream, I came to the conclusion that life is a parable in itself, with a vast supernatural array of meanings distributed across all time, space, and reality—from our past lives, into the present, and into all possible futures. Encountering Jennifer and Don felt like a wakeup call to me, reminding me that all answers come from within. We do not need to seek outside ourselves for spiritual help, as there are many resources that cost nothing and that will not drain us of our energy or compromise our connection with God and our Divine team.

If you are only seeking validation from a gifted healer who can see into the spirit realm and you are introduced to a trusted spiritual mentor, by all means, go for it. Just make sure you go in prepared to shield yourself, set intentions to connect with what is meant for you and your highest good, and never let anyone manipulate your energy to aid your spiritual growth unless you intuitively feel the approval of your higher self. Ideally, you will find a trusted mentor who will be honest in answering all your questions or concerns and who has no ulterior motives.

Our world is going through an extraordinary shift, full of revelations. The New Age is among us, but with the extraordinary epiphanies are deeply confused and twisted values and belief systems. Many unconscious people have treated the earth and the wisdom of the spirit realm as our possessions over hundreds of years in order to make a buck or two and to wield power over others.

It's OK to release preconditioned false beliefs and allow God and His universe to reset our lives individually, so that we can co-create a new reality. Our preparation for the Christ consciousness of oneness with the Divine will be helped by our awareness of our relationships with one another (including our karmic relationships), our daily connection to our alignment with the Divine, and our attunement to ourselves regardless of our religious backgrounds or belief systems. At the end of the day, I'm finding it important to simply surrender to the creator when we are caught off guard with health issues or challenges that could be linked to past-life energy or karmic attachments that may not be aligned with our life purpose. We have the ability to call upon the hosts of Heaven to intervene when needed.

We have nothing to be afraid of, and we must always remember to protect our energies before leaving the house after prayer and meditation. Love has no fear. We have complete control over our own energy, and we need not relinquish our power to people who will try to take advantage of us. Essentially, nobody has control over you. The only space you need to leave is for the Divine love that is your birthright.

CHAPTER 11

The Prayer Is in the Energy

"O God, who by the immaculate Conception of the Blessed
Virgin Mary, did prepare a worthy dwelling place for your son,
we beseech you that, as by the foreseen death of this, your son,
you would permit us, purified through Her intercession, to come
unto you. Through the same Lord Jesus Christ, your son, who lives
and reigns with you in the unity of the Holy Spirit, God, world
without end. Amen." —*Prayer for the Immaculate Conception*

By the middle of 2016, I was being intuitively guided to open up to the world of energy healing, particularly via Reiki, a system of hands-on healing in which universal energy is channeled to trigger emotional, physical, and spiritual breakthroughs. I could sense that the Divine was continuing to present me with people and situations that needed healing,. I was cutting and styling hair for a living, but I knew that those who came to me for that purpose were coming to me for so much more. The empath in me took it to heart when people sat in my chair and shared their life stories—and sometimes, instances of great pain, trauma, loss, and frustration. It often felt that God was speaking through my clients to me, encouraging me to help in whatever ways I could. Often, at night, I would take those clients who had entrusted me with their stories into my heart and prayers.

One weekend, my husband and I, along with my youngest daughter Jessica, were invited to a friend's house for a party. We ended up staying later than usual—the men enjoying a poker game at the kitchen table while the women sat and chatted in the living room. Out of nowhere, a woman named Kate, who was more of an acquaintance than a friend, began talking about her long-standing battle with infertility. "I've been off the pill for six months, and I've been taking sleeping pills in order to sleep and get my mind off this," she told us sadly. By the end of the night, I felt drained and helpless on her behalf...but wanted to do something on her behalf to help alleviate her worries, even though I didn't really know her.

So that night before bed, I took it upon myself to set positive intentions and to offer an intercessory prayer on behalf of her and her boyfriend. I could tell that they were both financially and emotionally stable enough to bring a new life into this world. As I bowed my head in prayer, I said, "Thank you, Father and spirit, for blessing this lovely couple in their relationship. If you feel it is right, then I ask that you leave a sacred space for a newborn to enter, all for their highest good. In Jesus' name, I pray."

A few weeks later, my husband and I were once again invited to attend a friend's celebration at a lounge in town. At this point, I was no longer drinking alcohol, as I experienced an unwanted mental and emotional haziness when I was under the influence. But I offered to go along and be the designated driver. As soon as we walked into the lounge and I saw Kate's face, I knew that she was pregnant. I sensed she had some exciting news to share, not only because of my intuition but also because she was quite visibly not drinking.

Sure enough, shortly after we got there, she made the announcement. "I'm around 11 weeks pregnant!"

Without censoring myself, I immediately said, "It's going to be a little girl."

"How do you know?"

I just smiled. "Well, let's just wait and find out."

As everyone began to gather and mingle, I found myself withdrawing from the physical realm as I began to reflect upon a message I was receiving: "Your prayers were granted." In the midst of all the people, I felt a wave of sacred gratitude coming over me. If only Kat and her boyfriend knew what had taken place behind the scenes! As I sat there, I had the urge to calculate the prayer date on my cell phone. As I did so, going all the way back to that first conversation in our friend's living room, I was delighted to see that everything added up. I knew in my heart that her conception was influenced by my healing intent to help her. All doubt was pushed to the side by this confirmation.

A couple months later, my family and I were invited to Kate's baby gender reveal party. She was at approximately week 19 in her pregnancy. As the couple cut into their cake, everyone got a glimpse of the pink frosting hidden within the layers. We all clapped. Just as I'd known without knowing so many weeks ago, it was a girl!

Kate's miracle continued to stay with me. In December, a few months later, I had a prophetic dream visit in which I came face to face with a beautiful baby. I knew that it was Kate's daughter. She showed me both her mother and her father, who had been extremely supportive to them both throughout Kate's pregnancy. Out of nowhere, an enormous jar of peanut butter popped up, as if to signify Kate's pregnancy cravings. The baby continued to communicate with me through symbols and ideas. She also shared that she wanted her birth to be photographed and every moment of her coming into the world captured so that her parents could later reflect on it with joy and wonder for their wedding to come. She then took me to the delivery room, all the while reassuring me of how much she loved both her parents, and how happy she was to have chosen them. Finally, she displayed herself born and placed on her back onto a hospital baby bed. She was a gorgeous, healthy-looking baby whose features were a combination of her mother and father.

How could I tell Kate about what I'd witnessed in my dream? I barely knew her! I felt it was important to share this message, though—but before offering it, I said a quick prayer, crossed my fingers, and intended it to be for her highest good.

She didn't know too much about my prophetic dreams, so she was shocked to hear about it. "This is wonderful, Cindy," she said. "Because it's my first child, I've been a little stressed about my due date and the delivery. I'm afraid my little girl won't be healthy. I can't believe you got to see her before me!"

My message gave Kate a glimmer of hope...especially because she was, indeed, craving peanut butter every day and had just restocked.

Early morning, on February 25, 2017, I received a private message from Kate announcing that the nurses had just induced her, and she'd been told that she'd have her baby girl early the next morning. I couldn't help but share what I was feeling—I reassured Kate that if she wasn't born during the day, she would be born that evening. That following morning, I woke up with a dream that her baby had just been weighed, inferring that she had already been born. As I opened my private messages, I was overcome by tears of joy. There she was—the baby girl I'd seen displayed in my dream vision just a couple months ago! And as I'd predicted, Kate had given birth to her the evening of February 25.

Since giving birth, Kate seemed to avoid me, although she politely suggested that we meet up every time we accidentally bumped into each other in the neighborhood. But there was no follow-up to these suggestions. I dismissed her avoidance with understanding, and a year passed. Then, I saw her daughter in one of my dreams again. This time, the message she shared was that her mom, Kate, was thinking of going back to work because her now-fiancé had lost his job. I prayed on their behalf and briefly messaged Kate to let her know that I was picking up on this energy in their situation, and that she and her family were in my thoughts. She immediately replied, half in disbelief and half in wonder: "That's crazy! He was just let go recently, and I've been thinking of taking on some part-time work as a waitress."

From this experience, I knew that whether or not people were ready to accept my visions, everything I saw came from source. Being someone who wore my heart on my sleeve, I had to admit that it was frustrating when I witnessed people in disbelief, as I knew that God's grace was limitless. There is a higher intelligence who deserves respect for its efforts beyond the veil. But regardless, I knew I was honoring my Divine role, and my loving efforts had impacted this family in a positive way. I didn't mind not getting credit for my insight—I simply wanted to pass along the beautiful blessings so that others could find reassurance in them...especially in times of hopelessness and despair, when they were needed most. I knew there was no greater gift than witnessing and being part of the miracles of the unseen.

In that period, I also received a dream vision in which my deceased stepfather showed up in spirit to tell me: "Cindy, you have the power to crack the code of conception." I had no idea what he meant. A large monitor with a running roster of numbers, almost like a stock market screen, popped up. An image of two other friends also came up, and the dream ended.

Are my prophetic dreams random, after all? I wondered.

It wasn't until later that I would discover that they, too, were trying to conceive, but had been unsuccessful. When I confirmed this information, I messaged one of the women, an acquaintance we knew through my husband, and asked her to come over for a healing or to be prayed over, but she refused. Although I knew I could be an intercessor, I also knew that it was pointless unless people were coming to me from their own free will.

At this time, another client (whose breast cancer I would later help to heal) told me that a friend of hers was having trouble conceiving. I decided to pray on her behalf after receiving the go-ahead to do so. She contacted me to tell me that she had felt her abdomen move, but because she had been having difficulty with IVF for years, she wasn't sure anything would work for her. Several months later, my client told me, "By the way, my friend whom you prayed for ended up getting pregnant. Just to let you know, she miscarried."

I could feel the pain of her loss, so I decided to pray for her again. By this time, my client had informed me that the IVF company she'd been working with told her she had a zero percent chance of conceiving. But she wanted a child so badly that she persisted. After another round of IVF, the woman became pregnant with twins!

I had the sense that my sending of distance healing prayers was deeply connected to helping women overcome infertility. Could this be a blessing in disguise?

I also began to reflect on the increased challenges that so many women seemed to be having around fertility lately. I could sense that in this time, too, many women—especially those who longed to be mothers—were allowing the darker forces of low self-worth and illusory thinking to get the best of them, to the extent that it was taking over their physical bodies. I knew that intervention could help, because healers hold the ray of God's love and light, which has the power to flush out darkness if others are open to receive Divine love and go through the purification process. Of course, there are many who don't understand that they have even been affected by external and internal negativity—and from my experience, many of them don't want to even think about it. But as an intuitive healer, I know that being of service to others is part of my mission of helping one soul at a time through God's abundant love. The more people we can help, the more these people will later help us as we transition into the spirit realm—if they happen to transition before us.

Never underestimate the power of your service to others; by unselfishly offering yourself as a channel of God's love, you open up to the universe's many pathways of guidance and support. In God and His spiritual entourage, all things are possible. When your mind, body, and soul absorb this truth, you will directly experience life's magical miracles.

I came to understand my connection with Kate's baby girl by way of recognizing that birth and death are portals to the spirit realm. Communication with unborn or deceased souls is possible because they exist in a state between physical and spiritual form. The notion of a beginning or an end is a social construct that we've absorbed. But in truth, we are all constant, continuous, infinite. We never begin or end—we simply transform.

All things are possible with a strong belief in the mysteries of faith in this multiverse. Although it can be challenging for some people to make sense of these mysteries and miracles, our minds need not comprehend what is occurring. We can place judgments of separation and pride to the side, and simply honor and acknowledge the blessings we are given. Intuitives who offer us powerful messages use a lot of effort and energy to spiritually help us.

We can all intercede on someone else's behalf if that someone is spiritually misaligned or disconnected from the Divine. We can simply be of service to others through a distance healing prayer, lifting up the situation to a higher power. When we pray by our mouths in spirit, it manifests in the physical world. Healing energies from a heart space radiate sacredness and conquer any darkness that one might be battling.

The more you gather in His name, the more potent the healing becomes. Be kind to one another through it all, because ultimately we are all given the credit we are due at the end of each journey. And remember, no prayer remains unanswered.

CHAPTER 12

Expected Intentions Create Manifestations

"You have an entire team at your disposal, archiving your life, your goals, aspirations, your thoughts and desires. Their sole purpose in existing is to help you become the very best version of yourself. That's what it's all about." —*Akasha Unleashed*

"It is no longer I who live, but Christ who lives in me." —*Galatians 2:20*

Growing up in my older years and throughout my marriage, I occasionally bumped into celebrities here and there when I least expected it. Many years ago, I found myself in Los Angeles at the age of 12, back when I had aspirations of becoming a model. I was on the trip with my agency and arrived at LAX for the first time.

I got into the hotel elevator after checking in and descended to the main lobby; halfway down, it came to a halt. A tall older man walked in. I could've sworn I had seen him on television but I couldn't quite put my finger on who he was. I had a hunch that he was Victor Kiriakis, from my mother's favorite soap opera, *Days of Our Lives*. I instantly felt intimidated.

"You must be here for the auditions," he said.

I responded with a quick nod and smile.

"Good luck," he said as he exited a couple floors before we got to the lobby. As I finally reached the lobby and as soon as the door opened, I took a step out. I was internally forced to stop. I heard a voice in my head say, "Freeze, then look to your left."

To my surprise, I saw what looked like an older version of myself sitting across a gentleman dressed in business attire. It looked as if we were in a meeting inside a lounge. And instantly I felt as if I knew the layout of the hotel lobby like the back of my hand, as if I were a frequent visitor. Once the vision was over, I snapped out of it.

That was odd, I thought to myself and proceeded to the snack bar before my audition.

Today, I realize that the male actor in the elevator was Jon Voight. As for the vision of the older me, it felt like a prophetic vision that will perhaps come to pass now that I am older. Who knows? There's just something about Los Angeles that keeps calling my name....

My encounters with celebrities would continue to manifest in my adult life. In September of 2015, I spent weeks exercising the Law of Attraction, an epic topic that captured my attention when I picked up a book with daily positive affirmations. This led me to deep sessions of meditation and prayers, particularly when the house was quiet and I had the chance to reflect over a cup of tea at bedtime. My reflections would turn into visualizations of what I wanted to experience in my life.

One day, I decided that I wanted to be in the audience of my favorite TV star, Ellen, and to witness her show in person. I also mused that it would be fun to have a random encounter with a Kardashian, just for the fun of it. It wasn't something I would have actively pursued, as I preferred that such experiences be fun and effortless. I was inspired by how Ellen and the Kardashians had built their personal empires, and I thought it would be fun to be in their company.

Of course, simply putting a request out to the universe, from my experience, always bore dramatic results. Six months passed, and I received a call from the *Ellen* show announcing that our entry to be in the audience had been selected! I had heard and been told that if one wasn't local, it was hard to get selected. Some had been trying for years.

Being in California, where I also got to spend time with my oldest daughter Jasmine, and my two lovely grandchildren, was amazing—and just as fun as I'd imagined it would be.

On the way back home, I thought it would be pleasant to have a couple's weekend in my husband's favorite city, Las Vegas. By chance, a pop-up ad for trip specials to Vegas appeared online, so I figured this was a sign for us to take advantage of it. We ended up booking accommodations at the Mirage, since we'd never stayed there before and had always heard it was posh and extravagant. It definitely felt like an out-of-the-ordinary event, especially because the decision to go had been so spontaneous.

To our surprise, upon our arrival, there was an announcement that Kourtney Kardashian would be making an appearance at 1Oak Lounge to celebrate her 36th birthday the following night. I automatically took this as an opportunity to begin visualizing in extra detail. In fact, for 15 minutes, I sat down and imagined exactly how it would be to see her in person, as well as what it would be like to get into the spotlight alongside her. Fortuitously, 1Oak was located downstairs from our assigned room. And I'd received so much confirmation over the years that our intentions became our reality that I had faith that the night would end in our favor.

As the time approached, we hopped into the elevator and basically followed the signage that led us to 1Oak like a trail of breadcrumbs. As the arrows helped us navigate the maze-like lobby, at a distance we noticed an enormous line and a doorman with a clipboard. I frowned. Obviously, neither my husband nor I were on the guest list. My intuition immediately kicked in and I avoided the line completely, while my husband followed me like he was my shadow. He had no idea what I was up to.

"Excuse me," I said with complete confidence to the doorman, memories of being 18 and getting into a nightclub taking hold of me. "Can you add us to guest list?"

He gave me a quick once-over, and without hesitation, he turned from a doorman into a bodyguard and walked us right up to the entrance, handing us two free cocktail stubs. From what I understood, Vegas lounges typically charge men an entrance fee while favoring women (particularly attractive ones), but apparently, we'd bypassed all of that. At this point, I felt a force much greater than me taking the driver's wheel, and I was simply in the flow of it.

As we walked in, we got a couple drinks and decided to check out the DJ booth; right next to it were VIP booths with celebrity names embroidered onto the cushions. I'd never seen anything like it before. I took a deep breath and reminded myself to keep an open mind and to ready myself for receiving only the highest good. The setting was lavish, the music was great, and my husband and I were simply taking it all in. For two low-key Canadians, it definitely was not the norm. We didn't even consider trying to sit at a VIP table; apparently, we would need to buy bottles, and that was way too much liquor for my liking. So instead, we decided to ask some women at one of the tables if we could stand off to the side. My husband excused himself to use the washroom while I decided to stay to admire the scenery and simply enjoy the night as it unfolded.

Within minutes, the VIP booth in front of me started to fill up, as an entire entourage followed a man into it. Upon glancing at the crowd that was gathering, I looked away without making any eye contact—but it was too late! The man immediately strolled over. "Do you want to join us?" he asked, a friendly smile on his face.

I smiled back. "No, it's OK. I'm just waiting for my husband to come back from the restroom."

With the loud bass thud of the DJ's music, I wasn't sure if he'd heard me correctly because he was persistent. "It's OK! Just come on in and have a seat and wait for him here."

I shrugged and nodded. Why not? I took his invitation but kept off to the side, nursing the same cocktail I'd been carrying around with me all night. As the group was still settling in with their waitress and discussing which bottles to get, the man came over yet again. "When do I get to meet your husband?"

Just as he asked, my husband walked by, his jaw dropped in amazement. He looked at me with a question mark in his eyes, but before I could say anything, the man grabbed his hand and shook it in greeting. "Hey, hubby!" he said. "Come on inside and have a drink!" It was almost as if they were old friends. My husband looked confused as they started talking, but I could tell he was grateful for the invitation.

From a distance, I spotted Shawn Stockman and the Boyz II Men crew. Shawn and I caught each other's eye, and I immediately began waving. Could the night get any crazier? He waved back. At this point, it felt like I was having an out-of-body experience; everything just felt too good to be true. I almost wanted to pinch myself. Could this really be happening? I could imagine that there were lots of women out there who'd played the role of glamorous celeb hanger-on, but I wasn't that kind of person.

The DJ overrode my deep thoughts with a booming, "Califooooornia's in the hooooooouse!" Fireworks went off, and servers carried an enormous birthday cake in. I could see Kourtney Kardashian and her boyfriend at the time, Scott Disick, being escorted to their assigned seats approximately three tables over from us. As the music pumped, I decided to stand up and walk across the landing between the tables. Now I was only two tables over from Scott and

Kourtney. Scott abruptly grabbed the mic from the DJ and burst out, "Who wants to personally wish Kourtney a happy birthday?"

I noticed a large group of women swarming over to their booth, and I watched curiously to see what they were up to. But security ended up pushing them away. At that moment, to my amazement, Scott looked straight at me and pointed. My eyes went wide and I pointed at myself, as if to ask, "Who, me?" I was in shock, given that I hadn't even made an effort to be chosen when Scott asked the question. I turned around to make sure he wasn't pointing at someone else when I realized that the people around me were impatiently waiting for me to respond. All eyes were on me. I nodded and eventually made my way over. At that point, my husband was still chatting with the people at the first VIP booth but when he saw me, he quickly grabbed his phone and jumped over the

VIP tables like they were hurdles at a track event. "Hey, that's my wife!" I could hear him shout.

He proceeded to take pictures of me as I went up next to Scott and gave Kourtney my best wishes for the year ahead. It was a surreal moment. *So this is what it's like to live a celebrity lifestyle*, I thought to myself.

To be honest, I'd never had any kind of conscious desire for stardom, but that night was a prime example of what's possible when we recognize our self-worth and have the confidence to step outside of our comfort zone. Every single person has just as much right to take up space as a celebrity, and to imagine that they are good enough to rub elbows with the rich and famous. It is only our false beliefs that limit us. Celebrities or not, we are all storytellers: in music, writing, painting, dancing. Those who feel a greater calling in any of these honor their soul by ultimately surrendering to their higher power, and thereafter, they are Divinely guided to receiving opportunities to bring their Divine voice and messages forward, and to express healing energy in the world.

Regardless of how famous we are, we all have opportunities to contribute to each other's internal healing—and some have large-enough platforms to do this on a broad scale. The next time you watch, read, listen to, or admire your favorite celebrity, ask yourself how this is healing for you. Also, how can you tap into your own authentic God-given healing talents, just the way you are? There's always someone watching who is willing to offer you the opportunity to tap into your own unique energy.

No matter our circumstances, the power of our mind reveals that anything is possible. And because we are all energetically connected, we can use this fact to direct energy in different ways. We can do this in our choices, actions, and our behavior toward ourselves and Mother Earth. Once we bring awareness to our every thought form and action, and recognize that all of it is just energy, we can eliminate a lot of the confusion and negative thinking that keeps us stuck in "bad luck" and a sense of feeling like we will never fulfill our desires.

In our society, many of us see ourselves as individuals with individual problems. As a result, we carry our troubles alone and believe that we are isolated from one another, and that we are undergoing our lives in a state of aloneness. This is an illusion! The reality is, we are all part of a greater consciousness, a huge energy source that we can refer to as God, source, the universe, or whatever else we want to call it. At the end of the day, we are all walking each other home. And despite the seeming differences in our lives, every single one of us will transition from this earthly plane, choosing our experiences (as stated in our life contract plan prior to our incarnation today) whether we are a celebrity, the prime minister, a CEO of the largest firm, or the next homeless person one passes on the street. Bottom line: We all carry a healing message for another. We are healing agents for a much greater purpose. Once we place our creator first in everything we do, all else shall be orchestrated in Divine order.

Life is a manifestation of where you place your energy. Anybody can manifest what they want, but the question to start with is, "What do I want that will bring me true happiness?" Next, you must be clear, affirm how you would like a particular situation to work in your favor, and remain in a state of gratitude as you set your intention through visualization, prayer, and meditation—ideally, for 5 to 15 minutes in silence. Allow the positive feelings to move through you, and allow any Divine guidance to help you on your journey. Nobody is strong enough to do it on their own!

Choose to consciously set positive intentions and let go of the constricted, negative energy of limiting beliefs and your perception of how to get to the outcome. Remember that you are never alone—and you can forego those feelings of separateness and negativity with open-heartedness and love. Become aware of the energies you are receiving and giving out—and if you really want to manifest something, experiment with something small, as I did.

Have fun with an intention of your choice—and in the fifth dimension (in spirit) of your meditative state, allow yourself to be an energetic match for what it is you want by allowing yourself to experience the excitement of getting what it is you most desire, as if you already have it. Then, hand it over to the universe in gratitude and prayer, knowing that it is done, or that something even better will come to you. Again, let yourself be in this state for 5 to 15 minutes, which will ensure that you are in the fifth dimension of Heaven on earth, where all things are possible.

The Almighty is space, so fill it in spirit. Allow your visions to naturally arise from this state, and see and experience yourself in a state of fulfillment. Overall, trust that your intentions have been heard.

I didn't go into that night or the taping of the *Ellen* show with the desperation of a starstruck fan, but with the awareness that I was going to have fun, no matter what. And I would simply make the most of what was before me, and tap into the energies being offered. As far as the Law of Attraction goes, I believe that Divine energy was simply moving me easefully toward my intentions. I was going to have fun, and the universe was going to help. After all, God always wants what is best for us, and always conspires in ways that will fulfill our heart's desires. When we invite this energy in, it is sure to sweep us off our feet and even surprise us in the process!

Of course, it might not be your ultimate heart's desire to meet a celebrity in a Las Vegas nightclub, which is totally fine! Everyone is on their own journey, but we are all interconnected. I simply chose to be an energetic match to the experience I wanted, and to allow that sense of connection to occur seamlessly. I did this by handing my desire over to the universe and allowing it to flow back to me.

Now, here I am three years later, and my husband and I have made it as audience members on the *Ellen* show for the third time. I must be doing something right. If I can do this, so can you.

Keep in mind that the universe always wants to fully support you as long as it's for your highest good. What do you have to lose? Trust in it and know that what is meant for you is meant for you. And whatever the outcome, don't forget to say thank you. Be persistent, but know when it is time to move on to something else. And always remember, whatever we sow shall we reap. The best possible earthly experiences is part of our eternal life as a whole. Start checking off items on your bucket list. Practice makes improvement!

CHAPTER 13

Prophetic Dreams and Premonitions

"Dreams are today's answers for tomorrow's questions." —Edgar Cayce

"For I know the plans I have for you, declares the Lord, plans for welfare and not for evil, to give you a future and a hope." —*Jeremiah 29:11*

Many people don't realize there are approximately 39 Biblical verses about visions and dreams. I began to dive into the world of prophecy when I discovered that I was a prophetic dreamer. Almost every night, I have dreams full of visions and symbols that give me an indication of things in my environment I couldn't possibly have known about. Many of my visions are random precognitive dreams that sometimes offer warnings about the future, or about a person's health and well-being, and they can also include information about the present moment. Other times, I receive spirit visitations from deceased loved ones, for both myself and others. The night before a healing I'll be performing for another person, I can put in a Divine request for further insight as to why they are being sent. Often it gets revealed in my dreams and comes to fruition during or after the healing.

The Divine is ever-present and attempts to connect with us every moment of the day, but most often, we are just too busy in our lives to experience these universal messages. Usually, pride takes over, limited beliefs block us, and the head rules over the heart. When this is the case, healing needs to take place in order for us to receive such blessings. When we remove our masks, our egos fall away. We begin to live authentically, with open minds and hearts. Experiences occur magically, all of their own accord, without either our resistance or prompting.

There are various ways in which the subconscious mind helps us release the hold that our ego, doubt, and fear have over us. In dreams and visions, where our conscious minds have let go of their control, the spirit realm is able to penetrate our consciousness even more. Our soul leads us to the messages we need to know.

Over the years, I've recognized that it's important to keep a record of the dreams that carry important messages, for they are a compass to our soul and our connections to others.

One example for me occurred in July 2013, when my oldest daughter, Jasmine, revealed that she was pregnant. It was entirely unexpected. Jasmine was 20 years old—and although I had been a young mother and wouldn't give up my experience for anything, I wanted so much more for her than I'd had. Although I didn't reveal my concerns to her at the beginning, I worried about her financial stability and capacity to provide for a child, especially as she was in a fairly new relationship, and she and her partner were both young. Everything was happening too fast for me. My husband and I had just invested in a new home, and Jasmine had just financed a new car. I wanted to educate my daughter on the importance of financial responsibility and ways to build her credit so that she would eventually take over our townhouse and be able to rely on an asset that she could always fall back on down the road.

That night I went to bed, my head and heart full of unanswered questions, and I received the third spiritual visit from my dad. In my dream state, I saw a vision of a condo that was similar to the one my husband and I had just purchased. From a distance, I could hear my mother's voice emerging from the kitchen, talking about God knows what. All of a sudden, her voice became fainter and fainter, and my father's image appeared in the crack of the front door, which had been left wide open.

My father walked toward me and took my hand; he then led me to a couch in the living room, where I saw a small baby wrapped in a white blanket. He gently sat down next to the baby and laid his hand gently upon it. He looked at me and telepathically shared that no matter the gender or the cause, this baby was a gift from God. All I needed to do was accept the child into this world with unconditional peace and love, for it symbolized a greater good than our own. He then reassured me that he would always be there to take care of Jasmine and the child, and that I should not worry about earthly concerns, such as how my daughter would pay the bills!

Today, I am gifted with two grandchildren, Aaliyah and Gabriel! Aaliyah just turned five years old and started kindergarten, and Gabriel just turned four. Throughout, I've noticed how having babies has grounded my daughter and given her a sense of passion and purpose in life. Now, as a grandmother, I feel that it's my job to leave a positive legacy for them. Spiritually, as a family, we have been blessed. Although Jasmine lives far away, in San Diego, our connection is stronger than it has ever been. Spirit occasionally drops in and gives me news about what she and my distant family members are doing without her awareness, and because of the close bond I have with my daughter, she confirms everything for me.

I've also had dream visions of other family members, including my mother-in-law (whom I call Lola, or "grandmother" in Tagalog) who suffers from early-onset dementia. She retired at an early age after working for the government for more than 25 years.

As I've learned, dementia is a complicated illness, and it has no cure. Of course, God's miracles abound all around us, so it's certainly possible to reverse the effects to a certain extent. Throughout my healings and observations, I have noticed that the souls of dementia patients actually leave their bodies and visit the spirit world periodically. Hence, it's possible to see them totally present one minute, and tired and absent the next. Often, because they don't enjoy the process of coming back to this earthly plane, they get confused, frustrated, and angry. They don't understand that they are very gradually transitioning. Eventually, they get to the point where they simply shut down and leave for good.

In January 2016, I had a dream that Lola had been admitted to a hospital. The doctor came out to notify my husband and me that she had just passed. It was such unexpected news that we didn't know how to react. But just at that moment, Lola popped up in front of us in spirit and said, "What are they talking about? I'm right here!" as she tugged on her shirt as a way of proving her presence.

It's been almost three years since she visited me in that dream. She's still alive and kicking with her humorous self whenever she is present. But similar to my dream, she tends to slip in and out of her body. Just recently, I gave her an energy healing because I noticed that her body would sometimes go limp, all verbal communication would disappear, and she wouldn't be present at all. Upon her waking up from her session on the healing bed, I intuited that she didn't want to come back to her body at first, although she eventually ended up doing so. After she got up from the bed, she said, "Wow, that felt good! Where am I?"

After that experience, it was like seeing a changed woman. She was much more energetic and was even able to play ball with her granddaughter, Jessica. Her hand-eye coordination improved greatly, and she was back to her former jovial, joking self. It made Jessica so happy to see the lively old Lola she'd always known. But we knew that this burst of energy had to be short-lived. Now, she lasts a good two to three hours after every healing session.

In another startling dream, I found myself giving birth to a new baby, much to my surprise! In early 2017, I dreamt of being in a delivery room and pushing out a beautiful brown-skinned baby. Everyone in the room shouted, "It's a girl!" I was confused; given the child's dark skin, I knew she couldn't be mine. When I woke up, I immediately shared this information with my husband, who had been by my side in the delivery room in my dream. He just laughed, because the scenario seemed so absurd. I simply assumed that the baby belonged to one of the women I'd sent baby blessings to, and that I would be a spiritual godmother yet again. I was excited to receive some real-world feedback related to my dream.

Sure enough, a day or two later, my husband sent me a text message informing me that his boss had invited some of his colleagues out to lunch to share some exciting news. Right then and there, I knew. "Your boss and his wife are pregnant with a girl!" I texted my husband.

Sure enough, that was the case. My husband's boss broke the happy news to the entire team that he and his wife (both of whom had dark skin) were expecting...and eight months later, upon delivery, confirmed that it was a baby girl!

That year, I felt as if my spiritual transformation was getting deeper and deeper, and as I cooperated with spirit, I was receiving more and more confirmation of my gifts. During this time, I'd discovered a greater intolerance to alcohol. In fact, I'd found it difficult to consume alcohol since 2014. But one night, my husband and I decided to try a Mexican restaurant close to where he worked. To my surprise, he ordered each of us a glass of red wine. But after a couple sips, I immediately felt guilty. And a simple sniff of the wine made me feel light-headed. However, since it was our date night, I was inclined to finish what we had started. But as the night ended, I began praying for forgiveness. It didn't feel right to be drinking. Before long, I went to sleep, and I received a vision of gorgeous handwritten calligraphy, which formed in the empty space before me. It read: "God bestows His love for you." The ink was a deep, dark blood red, which reminded me of Jesus Christ and His infinite love.

I immediately felt comforted, but when I woke up, I asked my husband, "What does 'bestows' mean?" I wasn't familiar with the pronunciation, let alone the meaning of the word, at the time, but now I know that it means "to honor, or bless, with a gift." I took this as a sign that God didn't hold me with anything except unconditional love and reassurance.

We all are worthy of forgiveness and grace. This doesn't require figuring out every mysterious blessing, or believing that we need to be deserving of it. We can always take comfort in the knowledge that we are never alone. As believers, we are always taken care of. And those who find balance and are in alignment with their minds, bodies, and souls will be able to receive the supernatural language of peace and love.

Our dreams are personal parables for us, and any chosen prophet embodied with God's presence can access universal messages in their dreams—then they can use these messages to radiate love and spread peace. In our waking lives, even when we are connected to spirit, it can become all too easy to get swallowed up in survival mode. However, we are momentarily released from all defense mechanisms in the subconscious dream state, so God's visions and images can come to us even more easily than they normally would.

As I always tell the people I meet who inquire about my gifts that absolutely anyone can experience prophetic dreams and premonitions of love, in the form of guidance, warnings, and blessings. In the realm of spirit, we have the power to reverse negative premonitions and curses, as what is being revealed to us is offering us an opportunity to move into greater spiritual truth. Simply ask to remember, and you shall receive, right before you go to sleep. Receiving nudges from spirit—whether from Jesus Himself, angelic beings, or deceased loved ones—is a wonderful confirmation that you're on your path.

If for any reason you received a dream message that involves someone else you may know, but you can't seem to make sense of it, it's most likely symbolic. If you are still unsure as to the meaning, you can approach that person immediately and share what you saw in the vision. Be as detailed as you can be, for sometimes even the seemingly small details can offer insight and reveal vital information. Don't be surprised if that person you dreamt about is experiencing exactly what you were shown. When you awaken from your dream, give thanks by journaling about it immediately. Take a moment to go within in silence, and shed some love and light on the situation through a quick prayer, which is a gateway for you to help intervene on the other person's behalf.

The more you respond to your dream interpretations, the more you show spirit that you can trust in what is being shared, and the stronger your faith becomes. It's a win-win in that you discover your own personal partnership with our multiverse!

CHAPTER 14

Divine Signs

"Don't let the doubts of others ring louder than God's whispers to your spirit." —Tricia Goyer

"Whether you turn to the right or the left, your ears will hear a voice behind you, saying, 'This is the way; walk in it.'" —*Isaiah 30:21*

It can be frustrating to witness this abundant multiverse and what it is capable of doing when we don't limit our Divine selves. Frustrating, because so often we remain in denial about our own ability to co-create with spirit. But spiritual interventions and blessings occur every single day! And they are available not just to people who've taken the higher path of a spiritual calling, but to anyone who is willing to let the Divine within shine and completely surrender our flesh so we can learn to listen to our soul. All we have to do is reset our minds, open the door to our heart space, and be in flow with spirit. The universe will help us, but only when we allow it.

I know that many times, I've found myself in a self-doubting space, even after experiencing the connection between me and the spirit realm. But often, it's been challenging when I've recognized that not everyone is having that experience along with me—or if they are, they are afraid to talk about it.

Despite the fact that prophetic dreams and miracles have been totally "normal" occurrences in my life, I have often felt that I'm living in a different reality from those who are stuck purely in the physical realm—even when they witness the miracles of spirit firsthand! Many of us feel the need to rationalize these supernatural experiences through "logic." But remember, if you see what others don't, you will see what others won't.

In September of 2017, on my way home from picking up my daughter from school, I was feeling stressed and under the weather. I'd had an unpleasant turn of events with one of the mothers at school, who happened to be my client. Basically, my experiences in the last couple years had been that many people were intrigued when I told them that I honored my calling by incorporating healing into my hair services. Some of them were eager to learn more, whereas others kept their distance out of fear—even when they were curious. But on principle, I always shared my experiences with people when they asked. And it sometimes made for shared bonding, whereas other times it made for awkwardness—particularly among those who had no knowledge or little interest in spiritual awakening.

The woman in question was an acquaintance of mine, and she also came to my salon to get her hair done periodically. During the time that I was getting an attunement in Reiki Level II, I asked her, "Would you like to experience a quick treatment?" Although she didn't know what energy healing was, she was interested and said yes. Shortly after that quick 15-minute complimentary treatment, something in her changed. She began working out more frequently and was motivated to take care of her well-being. I had a hunch that the treatment had provided some necessary clearing for her, but she never attributed the change to the healing session, nor did she ask for more treatments. I sensed that perhaps she wanted to, but simply wasn't ready or willing to go there.

However, something within her was responsive to the energy, although her conscious mind was resistant. At mass at our children's school, she sat beside me one particular day, and as we all started singing in unison, she began to tear up. "I feel the Holy Spirit around us," she explained. I wasn't surprised, as I felt the presence of spirit with me all the time. I nodded and smiled, but didn't say much more beyond, "Let's enjoy the moment."

In retrospect, I don't know if she was overwhelmed by her experience of brushing up so closely to supernatural experiences, but she began to avoid me over time. One day when I brought snacks for the kids after school, she seemed to go out of her way to avoid and ignore me. Although she talked openly with the other parents, she didn't so much as look at me. I found her behavior strange, even petty, but I decided that I wouldn't dwell on it. She also stopped coming to me to get her hair done. Although I was sad for the loss of our friendship, I couldn't help but feel that there was some internal conflict within her. Although gateways to the spirit realm seemed to be opening for her, she wasn't ready to walk through them. And most likely, I was a little too supernatural for her liking!

Although I resolved to keep my heart open and to welcome her with my friendship if she ever chose to come back, I was feeling sad and self-doubting one day, shortly after picking up my daughter Jessica from school. I was saddened by the reactions of people who chose to alienate me after I brought my own spiritual experiences to light. It was enough to make me wonder: Was I crazy? Not only did these thought forms bring my energy levels and vibration down, but my self-doubt had basically spoiled my morning.

I attempted to put the meaningless chatter out of my head and to snap back to reality as I talked to my daughter about how her day had gone. I chose to consciously release to the universe what I couldn't handle and took a deep breath as I basked in the feeling of the sun's warm rays coming through the sunroof while my daughter and I talked. We cranked the music, rolled down the windows to allow the warm breeze in, and proceeded to our next destination.

Just as we approached the traffic lights, my mind snapped back to the self-doubt that had taken over most of my day. *Am I actually crazy?* I wondered to myself. After all, I sensed the number of people who were unable to relate to my peculiar experiences.

Luckily, whenever I was in a state of not fully trusting the universe and all it was conspiring to show me, I always received signs that validated my experiences...that showed me I wasn't crazy after all!

As I sat at the traffic light, I felt a dream-like portal open in front of me, right in the center of the car where the rearview mirror hung. I saw an enormous, brilliant white feather approximately the size of my hand descend through the sunroof in slow motion, right in front of the mirror. It nearly obscured my sight when the light turned green, so I drove carefully. As the feather continued to float down, I realized that all of our windows were rolled down. So why didn't the feather just collapse and drift away in the wind?

Admiring it in silence, I simply watched it float in slow motion as it glistened before me and moved toward the window on the driver's side of the car. I considered reaching out to touch it, but before it even crossed the window, it disappeared before my eyes! I immediately looked over to see if it had bounced off the edge of the window, but there was nothing there. I also looked outside to see if it had flown into traffic. But there was nothing. Just as it had mysteriously appeared, it had vanished without a trace.

I immediately pulled over. I knew I wasn't just making it all up. After all, I hadn't been alone this time. I remained calm, cool, and collected as I slowly reached for my rear mirror and adjusted it down towards the backseat, where Jessica sat.

"Did you just see what Mommy saw?" I asked.

She nodded yes, speechless.

"What exactly did you see?" I inquired.

Like a deer caught in the headlights, jaw dropped as she held her popsicle out to the side, she proceeded to describe to me everything I had seen—including the large, brilliant white feather melting into thin air.

I began to cry tears of joy. I felt so validated!

"Mommy, are those happy tears?" she asked me.

I smiled. "Yes, they are."

As I realized that afternoon, the process of awakening is perfectly imperfect. There are ups and downs, trial and error...because that's all part of the spiritual tests that are given to you when you are on such a journey. And through my journey, I've come to realize that when I am feeling off or stressed out about something, the universe unfailingly comes to my rescue.

Universal signs come from anywhere and everywhere: through dream messages, people who directly address you with a healing message out of the blue, a song on the radio, coins that appear out of nowhere, odd-looking feathers, repeated numbers on billboards and signs, recurring numbers on license plates and digital clocks, and more. In a world that can sometimes feel chaotic, there are hopeful spiritual signs appearing all the time.

For me, the cherry on top was the fact that my young daughter had witnessed the type of occurrence that I often experienced when I was alone. In response to the question, "Am I crazy?" I had received confirmation that I could trust my senses completely!

When we move through awakening, the universe tries to get our attention and to prompt us forward toward our soul purpose. Even believers will wrestle with doubt, but the universe's loving signs help us to create space for internal knowing. In this space, there is no room for doubt, and miracles flourish.

I became aware that I had been allowing other people's fear-based thoughts and beliefs to encroach on my knowing and impact my own spiritual growth. But fear holds no power—in fact, it can paralyze us, and leave us feeling defensive, paranoid, and separate from source.

For me, this experience was a reminder that although we all come into the world with a similar mission (to move toward our soul's highest growth), we might come into this awareness at different times. After all, I know the number of people who thought I was crazy, only to come seeking me out after they'd received supernatural blessings of their own.

For those on an awakening journey, it's important to feel more and think less, detach, and send love and healing to others who are currently on a different path (and will eventually catch up when they learn to take responsibility for their own space).

Most importantly, we must set healthy boundaries so that we can create the peace we need for ourselves and continue to nurture our soul with unconditional love and self-confidence.. It can be a confusing and disorienting process, but it's important to find the beauty in all of it. We can do this by taking the path of least resistance and offering ourselves forgiveness when we experience negativity or self-doubt. We can ask for signs from the universe and learn to flow with our intuition with a clear mind and an open, sincere, heart that does not give its power away.

No matter what you are experiencing, the universe will always side with you and only wants the best for you. Through each experience, we learn more about ourselves. Not everything is sunshine and rainbows, even though many of us hope our journeys could be like this on a daily basis. It's vital to make a conscious effort to recognize the opportunities that are inherent in the bumps in the road and make the most of them. When you experience these bumps, take the next route. Remain in the energies you wish to receive. Stop and ask yourself and the universe, with the utmost sincerity: "Why is this happening?" Step back, reflect, and be on the lookout for universal clues on what to do and where to go next—and then, surrender. Ask that the messages you receive be clear and strong enough to grab your attention and ignite your intuition. Watch for random (yet orchestrated) internal dialogue that pops up with advice. Most of all, act on this advice!

Often, you will be led in a new direction, even if it means shedding unhealthy relationships, situations, and lifestyles. Give yourself permission to release all fear and all that does not serve your highest good or a greater purpose for all. Your experiences, over time, will generate greater strength, awareness, and wisdom—and will always move you out of the rut of self-doubt.

CHAPTER 15

Faith, the Silent Healer

"Through spiritual maturity, you will see new ways to avoid unnecessary suffering, wiser ways to endure unavoidable hardships with grace, and opportunities to turn you or pain into lessons of service and healing for others. Your hard journey has had a great purpose! Your pain was always a part of the plan to open your heart to love. Have faith. A miracle is happening in your life; the miracle of pain is transforming you to your higher self." —Bryant McGill

"And this is the confidence that we have in Him, that, if we ask anything according to His will, He heareth us; And if we know that we ask, we know that we have the petitions that we desired of Him." —*John 5:14-15*

During the process of my baptism, I was drawn to healing work that was directly about the laying of hands—a form of energy healing that I recognized as being sourced in Christ energy. My studies and my research led me to Reiki, a Japanese form of energy work that moves energy through the body and in and around the field surrounding the body. Although I came across a number of energy healing modalities—from Bioenergy to Pranic Healing to Matrix Healing—I was intuitively drawn to the simplicity of Reiki. I also knew that just because something was "complicated" and included multiple levels of learning and certification, that didn't mean it was effective. We don't need certificates to heal ourselves and others—we need open hearts that allow us to be channels for Divine energy.

Even before I completed the Reiki levels, I knew that I was gifted in healing others through intercessory prayer. I had already concluded that my God-given gifts exceeded what Reiki or any other energy healing course could give me. Although I knew that Dr. Mikao Usai's Reiki teachings were powerful, I was resistant to the idea that I needed to "prove" myself to other people in order to deem myself worthy as a healer. I didn't want to be the kind of person who found a sense of superiority by investing in a "mastery" course or putting extra credentials by my name. Although I valued the inner wisdom of "experts," as well as the teachers and spiritual guidance that had come into my life over the years, I also knew that my ultimate source is the sacred guidance of my own Divine soul team.

Still, I knew that it was wise to build on my skills and gifts in practical ways and trust that whatever healings took place spoke for themselves. We are all gifted healers and have nothing to prove to others. I wanted to free my mind and heart so that I wasn't operating from a place of fear, but from a place of love and true, dedicated faith.

My intention in seeking out alternative forms of healing was to dispel any fear-based illusions that had held me back from fully tapping into Divine guidance. For too long, I'd seen how people like my mother allowed their superstitions about what was "holy" versus "evil" limit their understanding of Divine nature. Sure, with light there is dark—but when we cast out darkness, it has no power over us. We are always safe where we don't relinquish our power.

I didn't want to be like my mother. I wanted to connect with everything that resonated with me along my journey, and to access any of the tools I'd been given that would help me to be of service to myself and others. Of course, it took a great deal of trial and error to find my way to those resources because I wasn't creating the time to internally listen to the silence of peace. I had to dig deep, pay close attention to my intuition, eat clean (this was a hard one), stay hydrated, and listen to all the clear universal messages being presented to me. Had I known this from the beginning, I could have simplified my life greatly!

I recognized that it was important for me to move through my early conditioning. After all, my mother had been an alcoholic who was more dedicated to her addictions and to her position as victim than she was to recognizing the support of her Divine soul team that surrounded and intervened on her behalf and created supernatural miracles. And my father had had little say in my upbringing and little understanding of me as a quiet, sensitive child—and one who'd clearly held spiritual gifts at an early age that might have blossomed freely had I not been shut down left and right.

As an adult, I was able to reflect on how numb and closed-off I had been at a tender young age. It had always been hard for me to ask for help when I was growing up, because I discovered early on that the answer would most likely be "no." I had little choice, which meant I had no voice. From my earliest years, I had learned to freeze most of my life energy in my first chakra, the energy center that represented survival and safety mode. This impetus came from the feelings of abandonment that left me with the awareness that the support I needed wasn't there. In some ways, it was better to not even acknowledge my own potential and gifts, but to simply focus on meeting my most basic needs.

In that sense, I, too, had inherited my parents' fear-based energy. I had learned that I couldn't simply turn to universal support to take care of my needs. I had to rely on myself...or better yet, have no needs at all!

While my connection to spirit evolved dramatically as an adult, it was almost as if that fear dampened the God-given gifts of my soul—everything that I'd come into this earthly plane to live and breathe—when I was a child. My gifts lay dormant, as I unconsciously allowed myself to shut down and shut myself off from spirit, just as my parents had. When I look back on that time now, I have compassion for my younger self, but I also recognize that if I'd known then what I know now, I'd be so much better off. (How many of us can relate?)

As I progressed on my spiritual path, I recognized that there were many unconscious stories I'd absorbed that I needed to return to their rightful owners. I decided that I would meditate and heighten my vibration to the fifth dimension. I envisioned myself at the age of 5 and my father at the age of 47. I invited his spirit at that age to accompany me as I gave him back his "earth stories," which had had nothing to do with me. "Your beliefs about spirit were your life lesson on this plane, dear father," I said, "and they have nothing to do with me. So I am giving them back to you so your soul can evolve for your next life cycle and so that I can grow spiritually."

I could sense my father lovingly reabsorbing those stories, as they exited my system. But I couldn't say the same for my mother. Now in her 70s, she has outlived her significant others and is more entrenched in her false three-dimensional belief systems than ever before. So I appealed to my brother in spirit and asked him to bring forth the spirit of my late dog, who carried a distinctive maternal energy. I asked her to take back my mother's earth stories, which I'd absorbed so deeply at a young age that I'd shut down my spiritual capacities altogether.

In sending these stories back to my parents, I was free to receive healthy masculine and feminine energies that would enable me to fulfill my true destiny so that I could heal and evolve. In this way, I recognized that it was possible to detach from the negative beliefs that abounded in three-dimensional reality and attune to universal guidance. I could finally see myself as a vessel of love and positive energy, no matter what I'd been taught at an early age.

During the sessions I offer to those in need of healing, grounding, and rebalancing, I have discovered that most of them are craving their own soul evolution and seeking universal messages pertaining to their own journey outside of church or their home. As a spiritual intercessor and a healer in partnership with God and my Divine soul team, I invite God and His universe in to help my clients receive answers to the intentions they bring with them before each session, all for their highest good. Ultimately, the outcome is God's ultimate decision. The living spirit knows best. Each healing session with me acts like a "purification reset" (similar to cleansing away our sins in a baptism), eliminating blockages often created by dark attachments that come about when we don't know how to protect our own souls.

Some of my clients have the option to choose to reconnect with their deceased loved ones, especially if those loved ones orchestrated the session behind the scenes to get closure or share insights about their transition process to the afterlife. By the end of the client's session, they release all that no longer serves them in the here and now. Opening the Heavenly realm within this earthly plane, I help cut ties to genetic curses (attachments) and end cycles that may not be serving future generations while praying for a complete restoration of my client from head to toe as they allow themselves to receive, feel, and release through their emotions. They also release fears linked to past lives, false illusions, and conditions others may have burdened them with.

I specifically work on all seven internal energy centers within each soul who comes to me. I have agreed to be in partnership with celestial beings, such as God, Jesus, guardian angels, deceased loved ones, ascended masters, and other spirit guides. I envision my client surrounded by a brilliant healing light that bestows enlightenment, intuition, wisdom, communication, hope, energy, vitality, desire, power, sensuality, intimacy, and security. I have come to cherish the moment when their sessions come to an end and they take their time as they sit up to collect their thoughts. I can see in their eyes that they recognize their soul purpose with an uplifted heart after a much needed healing purge. I especially love it when they make a conscious effort to make a difference in the world moving forward. When the life-changing testimonials flood in and their set intentions come to fruition, I know I've done my part. It warms my heart and makes me feel that I am witnessing God's celestial blessings!

As I heal others, I heal myself—and together, we heal each other.

As I also discovered, it's possible to have dreams in which spontaneous energy healing occurs. Once, I had a dream in which my mother popped in. We seemed to be sitting in a large audience at some type of circus setting. During the intermission, a group of acrobats invited people onto the stage to perform. My mother eagerly made her way down, much to my surprise. She was so determined to make her presence publicly known, even though she was much too old and out of shape. When she climbed a ladder, she immediately lost her balance, slipped, and fell. My heart dropped and I stood up, immediately running toward her. She fell through a thin net and landed on her head but slowly made her way back up. I was surprised that she'd survived the fall and could see that her body was covered in bruises. She turned to me and said, "Cindy, please heal me in the name of Jesus." I prayed over her twice.

After waking up from my dream, I called my mother to share my vision, almost expecting her to tell me that something had happened to her. Sure enough, my words were met by an awkward silence. "Cindy, my sister and I got into a physical altercation. I was beaten up, and my head is throbbing."

I nearly dropped the phone, shocked and disturbed to know that her dysfunctional relationship with her sister had persisted well into old age. Although my mother was set in her ways, I realized that her body had been in such pain that it led her soul to cry out to me for healing in my dream state. I hadn't even known such a thing was possible!

I understand, however, that when we send healing energy toward others, they are often answered with miracles. Whenever my daughter and I are out and about and we hear ambulance sirens, I call upon God and His angels of healing, light, and comfort. If the people who have been hurt are having near-death experiences, they can actually hear the prayers that come through. Then, if they are meant to return to this earthly plane, they will, but with a Heavenly memo attached that they help humanity and Mother Earth —and even if they don't return, the prayers will still help them with their transition to the next realm. I know that one day, I too will find myself in the same predicament in which I could use some healing prayers. So I choose to pay it forward and be a silent healer, even from the comfort of my car. I like to think that all of us are earth angels, and that the more we can pray for others and walk with an open heart, the more we can engage in healing

I also enjoy saying silent prayers for strangers I pass, especially the homeless. In a session with a past-life healer, I received the insight that I had been homeless in a past life, and that I had purposely chosen that lifestyle because I wanted to be an example to others of the power of humility. Today, I never pass a homeless person on the street without giving them money, food, warm clothing, and/or intercessory prayers if I have nothing else to offer. Something about them manages to strike a chord within me, and I am reminded that every single one of us, no matter our station in life, has the capacity to walk with God and to be in partnership with our Divine energy to serve our soul purpose.

There are many techniques that one can follow to heal someone, and often, they will reveal themselves in unexpected ways. Often, healing can occur through dreams, prayer, or even using a tool that you've been universally guided to, in order to align with higher energies of love and light. These tools might be the Bible, singing bowls, a pen on a notepad, angel cards, crystals, pendulums, or other objects—all of which are perfectly, Divinely orchestrated to help us carry out our soul missions. As long as there is a clear and positive healing intention, breakthroughs will occur.

As eternal beings having a human experience, we are blessed with organs, muscles, senses, and energy centers within our bodies—not to mention our intuition, which helps us navigate through life whether we are aware of it or not. We are all born channels of God and His Divine team. Such gifts are natural, and also free! (Just be sure to release and visualize a green healing light upon your adrenal glands, located above your kidneys, every once in a while, as this will boost your energy and emotions!)

Healing is common among all religions and spiritual paths, but the laws of universal healing state that a request for help must be present in order for healing to occur and to effect meaningful changes. Then, healing can occur through contact or distance, or simply focusing on the aura of the person being healed.

We are all created in the image of Jesus Christ in mind, body, and soul. Jesus contained the father, the son, and the Holy Spirit—and this highest universal energy flows through all of us—as we are all pieces of the whole. Energy healing allows us to regain control over our lives, especially when we may have allowed dark shadows in and require surrender back into our childlike faith.

A new reality is currently among us. If you are reading these words, this is the time to find healing modalities to quiet the mind and allow yourself to surrender to the higher power. May we never forget to thank the one to whom we owe everything. The greater our personal relationship to God, the more powerful the confirmations of our Divine origins will be. Through unconditional love, humility, expanded awareness, and compassion to ourselves and others, you can open up to faith in the universe. You can be healed and fully supported in your soul purpose.

CHAPTER 16

Dimensions and Beyond

"The cosmos was formed according to and upon the basis of laws which are expressed as music, arithmetic and geometry; they bring out harmony, order and balance." —Edgar Cayce

"In the beginning God created the Heavens and the earth." —*Genesis 1:1*

Through my research over the years, I have always wondered why people seem to be awakening at different times rather than all together. I've also wondered what dimension one must be in to experience certain milestones in their spiritual growth. It may not even truly matter, but it's important to be aware. We are all operating in different dimensions of reality, even if we do not consider ourselves spiritual.

Dimensions are not places or locations, but levels of consciousness that vibrate at a certain rate; the higher the vibration, the more dimensions we consciously experience. In meditation, we are able to access wisdom from the highest energy source—which I like to call the throne of God.

During my spiritual awakening, all the memories of everything that played out in my life as a child flowed back to me. Ever since then, it's as if I see life from a bird's-eye perspective. As I observe people asking questions like, "Why did this happen to me?" when confronting unexplainable events. I notice that for myself, answers come from a place of simply knowing the possibilities of why it happened—all through my awareness of the various dimensions. I needed to understand the basics of these dimensions in order to make sense of my own experiences—since none of this information was shared in spiritual classes I took. Thus, I undertook research into the many characteristics of the third, fourth, and fifth dimensions.

Unfortunately, many people who are closed off to meditation and prayer might not believe in anything greater than their three-dimensional reality. Often, they are consumed by the details of the mundane world and remain unconscious to anything else. But when we are not aware of anything beyond this 3D earthly plane, we are not aligned with our true selves.

Sometimes, people experiencing third-dimensional reality enter the fifth dimension; in this place, they often feel disheartened and lonely, as they are able to see a world full of pain, suffering, and feelings of helplessness. This is when spiritual healing could actually benefit them most—otherwise, they might find themselves caught in a cycle of despair that smothers their soul evolution and could end fatally.

It is quite possible to expand into multiple dimensions of consciousness simultaneously, but this isn't for everyone. When we are stuck in conditioned belief systems, limiting religious ideologies, and the like, it isn't always possible to move from a 3D physical reality to a 5D Heavenly perspective; in fact, it simply won't work to do so unless the person in question is aligned with the frequencies of the fifth dimension. If we are witnessing a friend who is stuck in the third dimension, we can learn to support them with patience—especially if they are not hindering our own spiritual growth. Whatever the case, it's wise to build healthy boundaries for our own well-being and allow those around us to have their own experience and be on their own karmic ride...as we all are.

We have all encountered some of the traits of living in a third-dimensional reality. These can include seeing oneself as separate from others and from the web of existence; judging others on the basis of their skin color, ethnic background, age, gender, financial status, and other superficial labels; seeking happiness outside of oneself, such as in material possessions, relationships, money, and physical attributes; and being opinionated and closed-minded in one's beliefs. The labels we create for ourselves in third-dimensional reality define who we are to such an extent that they ultimately limit us and our sense of reality—leaving us oblivious to the vast, evolving planet of information that it is possible to access.

Sometimes, people transcend their 3D reality through certain spiritual tests. For example, parents who have children with health issues are often prompted to grow and to open their hearts and minds through patience and unconditional love. Many of us are born into families that help our soul evolution so that we can all benefit.

However, if a soul is stuck in the 3D physical world, and with free will they made the wrong turn by not following their intuition or by resisting their soul growth, they can be taken abruptly from this earth realm. In this way, after transitioning to the spirit realm, they have the opportunity to come back to earth in their next life cycle so that they can be given another chance with the same life lessons—until they integrate unconditional love, oneness, patience, and compassion for humanity.

The fourth dimension is considered the realm of spiritual awakening. This is the realm where you know there's more to life than this land beneath our feet, but still, you are deeply aware of and sensitive to your surroundings. This is where the light of consciousness begins to awaken from within, and where you begin to assess third-dimensional belief systems and uncover their absurdity. This makes you wish to press the reset button on your reality and detach yourself from the world until you can figure out what it is you are experiencing.

Many people falter in their spiritual growth when they get to this stage. They might get caught up in feelings of anger, resentment toward society or their families of origin that implemented these belief systems, and their life circumstances. However, if they move through their feelings, this is where things become much clearer. Life is no longer linear, and there is an ongoing sense of simply being able to be in the present moment as it is. In the fourth dimension, we also discover the experience of time stretching and no longer being linear. Time might fly for us, and yet we might be able to get a tremendous amount of work done (I've especially found this to be true for myself lately). When we transition to 4D reality, we might still experience comparison and judgment in our 3D reality, but there will be a shift from the material world to greater knowledge and understanding. We will find ourselves more capable of moving beyond competitive ego states to create peace and harmony with one another, meeting each other where we are in our respective journeys.

This brings us to the fifth dimension of reality, which I refer to as unity consciousness, or creating Heaven on earth. At this point, earth angels will start to experience symptoms of the third eye opening up to its fullest. They will persist in states of oneness with the universe. They will find themselves existing in a place of joy, love, gratitude, and a deeper understanding of the external world. To access this space, it's best to release all emotional baggage and leave it at the door where fear, anger, hostility, guilt, suffering, or a sense of separation from God's magnificent universe exist.

The fifth dimension is also where we access the bounty of the Law of Attraction. By simply thinking of something, it presents itself to us—which is why it's crucial to keep our thoughts positive and think big, knowing with our heart of hearts that what we wish for will be ours. This is also where we access senses beyond the five senses, such as telepathy. It becomes possible to reach others simply through our thoughts and feelings. Many may experience vivid dream messages for themselves and others. And of course, from this place, there is no distinction between the past, present, and future—it becomes possible to access our past lives, as well as our future ones.

In the fifth dimension, we no longer strive to change the world or to save others; rather, we focus on healing ourselves from within and discovering the supportive tribe that resonates with us. We recognize that the darkness of the world is, in fact, a reflection of the shadow that still exists inside of us—and that love conquers all. Labels vanish, and we begin to see ourselves ever changing on a conscious level. We are more aware of our energy and where we are spending it. The judgments of others no longer impact us. When we come to access the master within, we eliminate fear and internal chaos, instead choosing to live an enlightened life.

Remember that we are all Divinely connected to one another through our DNA and through God's living spirit, no matter which dimension we find ourselves in. This is His true glory, a limitless gift from our creator to us.

Many tools exist for us to clear our energetic blockages through all time, space, and dimensions, allowing us to move more freely between the dimensions. For example, according to sleep prophet Edgar Cayce, the Lord's Prayer clears and restores our chakras and automatically raises our frequency.

We are all children of God and need to be aware of the energy we are putting out into the world, as well as whether it is depleting or energizing us. For example, when I sense that what I am about to share will not resonate with another, I try to support them by putting myself in their shoes, simply offering whatever I can in the hope that their soul will receive the message and they can later reflect on it. I also leave them an internal prayer for their situation, resting in my knowledge that God has it all under control.

Since I have agreed to honor my life contract by opening up to my spiritual gifts and devoting my time and energy to God's mission, He has opened up the spirit realm, orchestrating events before my eyes even before I am aware of them. Because I have no control over any situation that gets presented to me when I am Divinely guided and guarded, I act more as a vessel and learn to flow with Divine energy. All knowledge comes from a much higher source than our own, and it provides us with the guidance we need to fulfill our purpose in the world, according to a much greater and ever-evolving plan than we are aware of.

The global wave of higher consciousness is highly contagious and growing bigger and wider each and every day. We are all being called to reach our highest potential at this time. Many of us do not remember the other side of the veil, where the spirit realm abides. This is because the universal knowledge to which we had access before entering the earth plane was much too vast to comprehend, given the limitations of the 3D mind and body. Whatever we have learned in our past lives gets stored in our subconscious, often creating limitations in this lifetime due to past life experiences. For example, if we are fearful of heights, this might be related to the way we died in a past life. Today, we have the opportunity to overcome this fear when we raise our vibrations and awareness; when we find ourselves in the fifth dimension, as we hear spiritual gurus mention quite often, we remember some, if not all, of our past lives. We gain a keener understanding of our soul contract, which helps us better evolve our journeys, eliminating illusions and confusion.

Make it your conscious goal to learn to vibrate on a higher level, for when you master your frequency, you master your destiny. In order to shift with ease to match these transitional times, it's important to take care of your internal being. To honor the dimensions of your heart and soul, stay grounded; bring balance to your mind, body, and soul; and raise yourself up to the fifth dimension to eliminate the chaos of lower vibrations. Shield yourself daily so you can create the peace, joy, and love you deserve.

CHAPTER 17

Arise and Shine!

"Fact: When you raise your vibration, relationships, partnerships,
and friendships may dissolve. It represents the releasing of
karmic ties to the vibration you had when the circumstance or
relationship began. Through the eyes of the universe, the ending of
a relationship doesn't have to symbolize you being rejected, but can
be seen as a graduation out of an outdated level of consciousness
that such relationships helped you outgrow."—Matt Kahn

"Thou shalt also decree a thing, and it shall be established
unto thee, and the light shall be established unto thee, and
the light shall shine upon thy ways." —*Job 22:28*

Who knew that in four years I would be sitting here writing this
book and having an audience like you reading it? Being a first-
time author coming from a complex background such as mine—
not to mention being a total introvert and an above-average student who received average grades in English class—it's still hard to believe that I'm sharing
my story in this form.

The point is, everyone has a story to share and a purpose to contribute.

Sure, there will be others who may have more education or more experience,
but when you are being Divinely pushed beyond your comfort zone, you will

find yourself going places and undertaking endeavors that would not have been possible on your own. When we allow the universe to work through us, we are able to function in ways that may surprise even us. But we seldom do it alone. Together, we find that we are much greater than the sum of our parts. So instead of harboring jealousy for those who seem to be "ahead" of us, we can offer our heartfelt support—which can only lead to breakthroughs on our own journeys.

The process of committing my story to words began before I even considered writing a book. Visions and dreams of my future as an author bewildered me, and random spiritual teachers constantly inquired as to when I would write my book. I always responded, surprised, "Who...me?" My ego constantly intervened to tell me things such as, "You're not worthy...you can't write...you don't have an important story to tell." It took many attempts on the part of God and the universe to get my attention enough so that I could take action.

When we step out from behind the lies of the ego, we discover just how much power we have as souls. In fact, we were born with a celestial team of guardian angels, angels, spirit guides, deceased loved ones, and other beings who might sometimes deliver their messages of love and support through ringing in our ears, synchronicities, internal messages, and guidance. We are all on borrowed time, a God portion of time that allows us to grow and transform, leaving our healing vibration of energy in the world, even long after we have left our human form.

It was only in returning to my childhood dreams that I realized I had always harbored the desire to be a teacher and an author. As a young girl, I had envisioned myself sharing heartfelt stories with others, but I never actually took those visions seriously. I didn't understand that this was my actual calling. I have since learned that reflecting on childhood memories and dreams can offer one a sense of solid direction when they feel lost in the rat race. We only need to look back on those early days to find a sense of purpose and understanding that there is more to life than survival, or "working for a living." Simply think about what you were good at or what grabbed your attention when you were a child. What were your dreams and desires? With child-like faith, invite the universe in to help shine some light on this inquiry.

As I began to integrate those early recollections of writing and sharing my stories, and as more and more universal nudges revealed my purpose to me, I finally accepted it all. I put my pen to the notepad and found myself uploading and channeling endless universal transmissions. I would sometimes write for hours on end, often finishing a chapter with a sense of my head being stuck in the clouds. I often didn't want to stop. I found myself having to go back to re-read what I'd written, as if someone else had written it; often, I didn't even remember what I'd committed to words and what each chapter consisted of. I simply got out of my way and allowed my thoughts and my pen to take over. I simply trusted that source always finds a way to send us our soul purpose messages—especially if they are part of the greater calling for our highest good, as well as the highest good of others. I have often received random uploads followed by overwhelming sacred feelings out of the blue, which leaves me in tears of gratitude, reassurance, and joy at times. I am always sure to send the universe a warm energetic hug in return, and to open myself to even more.

If you are Divinely successful in doing the things you love and you are aligned with your true self, you will come to discover that everything will flow to you much more easily. And boy, does it flow! Life flows with magical abundance, as well as tests of your faith, every day. Unfortunately because everybody's energy varies, not everyone you meet will be happy for you—but just know that the universe is and that's all that matters. Do not allow others to feed you their insecurities, fears, worries, and doubts. The flesh illusions and shadows of ego need to be dismissed so that you can shine your light.

During this process of internal growth, we put aside the competitive ego and ignore those who carry these traits by default (it's their karma and life lesson, not ours). We forgive them as they are, send them blessings, set healthy boundaries for ourselves, place God first in all that we do, set positive intentions, detach from idolizing material things or thirsting for more, and convey our authentic message with clarity and trust.

It's inevitable that some things will test our faith, and karmic relationships may rise out of nowhere. We have to be patient with the process and also learn to energetically shield ourselves and sever etheric cords that tie us to other people. We must also trust in God and our Divine soul team and not try to control the outcome, but to simply keep challenging ourselves to be at our best. Through our failures and difficulties, we are stronger—we have already won!

Lately, I've been reciting a daily mantra that goes something like this: "Thank you for the hard lessons in the past, as I have learned from them and am now ready to receive the easier lessons in the now to help me in my future moving forward." Then, with a conscious intention, I continue to walk in love while illuminating Christ energies on the planet.

As a reminder, we are unlimited beings and deserve to give ourselves permission to be fully loved, internally happy, and prosperous as co-creators with the universe. This simply requires allowing our soul to shine above all else. (In fact, in partnered relationships, make sure the other person has fallen in love with your soul first, and your body last. This will determine the happiness and longevity of your relationship.) If spirit and the power of your thoughts and your words put you where you need to be for your Divine purpose to shine through, everything else will be set in place to ensure your success for humanity.

Don't worry too much about your finances, or allow self-sabotage to ruin your day. Simply enjoy the process of co-creating your destiny by taking control of the energies in your space, trusting in the process, and letting go of the outcome. Pay attention to your internal and external dialogue. The power of our tongue can create life, curses, and blessings—or lack, despair, and even death. We were born carrying the precious energy of language as commanding beings under the holy light of God our creator. It's time to give ourselves permission to step forth and alter our environment with the power of our choices, words, and intentions. The quality of our life is directly related to the quality and frequency of words we speak. Dr. Masaru Emoto and his experiments on the molecular structure of water demonstrated that human consciousness has an impact on all matter—including ourselves.

When we are on the path to claiming our soul purpose, it's so crucial to be aware of our free will and the choices we make. We must do our best to steer clear of lower-vibration relationships that bring us down and be strong in removing ourselves from gossip, judgments, or addictions that contaminate our sacred temple and prevent us from staying on our true path.

Said something wrong? "Stop, cancel and delete!" By reciting this immediately, you will erase the unwanted spoken words with love, releasing all ties that may be karmically related. Such preventative actions allow for peace, even if it means we need to become hermits and isolate ourselves from the external world for a short time to raise our vibrations and receive answers for the direction we need, to just be. You can absolutely say what you mean, but there is also great wisdom in internal silence.

Once we can fully be ourselves, removing and shedding all the masks and layers of scarcity mentality (which we most likely inherit from others), our internal light starts attracting abundance and magic on all levels. Our chakras align with our soul, as each energy center represents how we handle a situation in our life. Often, our energy centers are imbalanced, as we allow other influences to take over our peace and harmony. Once we allow our feminine and masculine energies in and find internal balance, we learn to manifest more easily and function more clearly.

The journey to manifesting your purpose always begins with considering how you can be of service. My advice is to be comfortable with self, heal from within, regain your strength, collect your thoughts, and stay focused. Who cares if no one is cheering you on in physical form as you arise and shine? I guarantee that you will feel lonely during your transformation, which is quite normal, but you are never alone. The universe is always conspiring on your behalf and has your back. There is no such thing as lack or impossibility in God's house.

We are created with unique healing talent and inner sacred messages to share with the world and in our communities, so what are you waiting for? If you can, take a moment to put this book down and grab a pen and pad of paper. Command greatness with your words. Stop, think (with your heart, not your mind), and put down in words what your soul wants. Take some time to read over what you write. Then, allow the grace of God, your guardian angels, and your guides to support you in action. Be inspired by those who are inspiring, detach from the outcome, and lead by example in your own unique way! Through love, you can make a difference—and don't be afraid to add a splash of humor while you're at it. Laughing raises your vibration, and better yet, it's contagious!

Remember: There is always a greater purpose for each of us, and it is unfolding behind the scenes, even in times when we are confused or bereft of hope. We all have a mission, and a unique way of being of service. We are all blessed with a healing energy that nobody can take from us, and it is greatly needed for the specific role of our soul occupation. If you feel the call to expand, go for it! Action eliminates fear, and whatever we seek it's seeking us. Take a risk, be comfortable failing, and appreciate the lessons. The more you get the hang of this, the more you will get to know your soul self and become stronger in your faith, as long as it's not bringing any harm to yourself and others, ask for Divine help and know that all will be well.

CHAPTER 18

Blessed by John of God

―――――――――――――――――――――

"Medium: A person used as a spiritual intermediary between
the living and the dead"—*Collins English Dictionary*

"A medium is a bridge, a translator between two realms. We are a
conduit of energy, bringing forth healing messages from beyond this
physical world. A healer and a friend to all souls." —Unknown

"For with God nothing shall be impossible."—*Luke 1:37*

There are moments in life when, without a doubt, you can sense that you are face to face with your destiny. This can include a spiritual calling, the birth of your children, or the fulfillment of a big dream. And often, it can entail a powerful affirmation of everything you know you are here on this earthly plane to do. For me, meeting the healer John of God was one of those moments.

After being approached by a client in 2017 to donate to one of her local clubs and to enter a raffle, I entered without hesitating or even knowing the cause I was contributing to. I was simply excited for the opportunity to give back. That evening, I received a call letting me know that I'd won a $2,000 travel voucher! I knew that none of it was coincidence. My family and I had moved in the last year and had also downsized our home. I knew this was a nudge from the universe to help me with my spiritual growth and to make the journey ahead easier.

I immediately asked God before bed that night where He wanted to send me. Two days later, I received a vision of seven huge, stunningly beautiful Vogel crystals, which are healing quartz crystals cut to the dimensions outlined by the findings of scientist Marcel Vogel. They hung in a rack above my healing bed. I was confused when I saw them, as I didn't even know that they existed. But I immediately assumed that perhaps this was a sign I needed to add hanging crystals above my healing bed.

As I came out of meditation, I grabbed my iPad and began to Google "healing crystals over massage beds." That was when, John of God popped up.

I'd never heard of him before, but as I read, I marveled over what I discovered. João Teixeira de Faria was a 76 -year-old man from Brazil widely known as John of God, a psychic surgeon. I learned that he had attended to and healed millions of people through crystal therapy treatment, as well as non-invasive spiritual operation with an option for invasive surgery for those who felt the need to experience the physical procedure because they had received pessimistic diagnoses from their doctors. But after people visited him at his healing center with life-threatening diagnoses or ailments and followed the prescriptions they received, many of them did the unimaginable: They healed. The pictures of abandoned crutches, braces, and wheelchairs at his shrine spoke for themselves.

John of God had been healing people for over 50 years, but he didn't take credit for these miracles. As he would often say, "I have never healed anybody. It is God who heals."

I read further and discovered aspects of John of God that I immediately felt a connection to. He'd grown up poor and was often hungry in his early years. He attended school briefly and never learned to read or write. He discovered at an early age that he had the power of prophecy, and could predict sudden and devastating storms. At the age of 16, John of God had a vision of a woman who gave him the address of a nearby spiritual center. After he went, he fainted and woke up hours later, and many people were gathered around him. To his astonishment, people told him that he'd performed healings that entire afternoon—none of which he remembered. Since then, John of God has been a medium who actively works with "Entities," a group of spirit beings who perform healings through him.

I also discovered that John of God was the creator of crystal bed treatment, which basically entails putting a client on a bed and hanging a set of seven quartz crystals above them. Each crystal is lit up in a different color to indicate a specific chakra and emits a special frequency that helps the person on the table walk away feeling restored and healthy.

I contacted the center in Brasilia, Brazil, immediately—and was told that John of God didn't send his sacred healing lights out to just anyone. "It's best that you come and arrange for your request to be approved by him personally," one of his assistants informed me.

That was it! Here was the answer to the question I'd posed to God just a couple days ago! *I'm supposed to go to Brazil*, I thought to myself in wonderment.

In the next several weeks I made arrangements for me, my husband, and my daughter Jessica to get on the plane and go to Brazil.

I knew that my husband was somewhat freaked out by the visions that had determined our "vacation," and that he was also wary of the notion of spiritual surgery. He couldn't believe that I wanted to go through with this, especially since it was so far from home. "Let's negotiate," he told me. "You can have one week with John of God, but I also want a week in Rio during Carnaval."

I agreed to my husband's terms, figuring that since he was being so easygoing about the whole thing, I could at least compromise. Everything I knew about John of God felt so aligned with my own sense of purpose. He had continually offered a powerful message of love, compassion, and hope for humanity. By allowing "spirit doctors" to take over his body three times a week to miraculously treat the thousands of people from all over the world who came to him in need of remedies, he'd helped to bring even skeptics closer to their faith.

Landing in Brasilia was humbling. It was my first time being outside of North America, and I wasn't accustomed to life in a third-world country. I didn't understand how the healing icon I'd read about could live in such a place...but over the course of the healing process, such thoughts subsided. My ego was replaced by the energies of unconditional love and compassion.

Upon arrival, we met up with our tour guide at our hotel, and we shuttled to Abadiania toward John of God's Casa. We noticed that our ears began popping as soon as we entered the area of his healing sanctuary. Our tour guide explained that this was due to the high healing frequencies and protection bubble that surrounded the region. "As soon as you booked your flight and agreed to receive healing from John of God, spirit doctors already began to work with you," she informed us.

It was a Monday that we arrived at the sanctuary. We were told that John of God conducted healings three times a week: Wednesdays, Thursdays, and Fridays. We decided to go to the place where we were staying, which was about a five-minute walk to the Casa, to get settled. It was February, which meant that it was rainy season in Brazil. When it rained, it poured for five to ten minutes, which would then be followed by bursts of sunlight. Whatever the case, I preferred it to the frigid weather back home!

The kitchen staff at our place of residence served patients of John of God three blessed, home-cooked meals daily. They also offered room service to those who received a spiritual operation and were confined for 24 hours after being healed at the Casa. Tuesday was our private tour of the Casa. I admired everything from the beautiful shrine, to the prescription dispensary, to the newly renovated washrooms that Oprah Winfrey had generously donated. Adjacent to them was a beautiful green healing space with wooden benches engraved with gorgeous hearts. A heart with the word "Jesus" caught my eye as we strolled by to the soundtrack of chirping birds, which led us to a verandah that overlooked a beautiful valley. All around, people were sitting in meditation. Once our tour ended, the three of us sat off to the side admiring the scenery, which felt like Heaven and earth were meeting. I fell to my knees and burst out crying, as the inner knowing that we were meant to be here hit me.

I was eager for Wednesday to come around, and when it did, I was incredibly excited. Those of us who were seeing John of God for the first time were led to a different line. On stage and in the reception hall around the Casa were friendly volunteers who would take the microphone to offer different prayers and information in many languages. Every single one of them had their own personal story of being healed by John of God and had chosen to be of service to humanity alongside him.

It was mandatory to wear completely white attire during the whole week or two of our stay; we were told that the spirit doctors needed to see through us in order to heal us as a whole. Upon entering the Casa doors, we were greeted by more volunteers who looked like nurses and doctors; they led us to the back, where John of God sat. A group of meditators sat with their eyes closed, raising the healing vibrations to help the Casa. This was known as "sitting in current." The current rooms were behind the main hall, and those meditating inside them were literally creating a current of love and prayer for the healing of all visitors. When you took your seat in the current room, you simply closed your eyes and didn't open them until the morning lines had passed before John of God.

I simply basked in the peaceful scenery, taking in the scent of lilies and lilacs, as well as the white hospital cabinetry and the enormous floor crystals and statues of Jesus Christ and Mother Mary. The entire place had the atmosphere of a warm, healing hospital—so unlike the regular hospitals I and too many others are accustomed to.

As we approached John of God with three specific intentions for our healing, the Entity he was working with that day scanned us, and then diagnosed what our soul needed for our highest good. My husband went first and was given a prescription for passionflower and a healing energy meant just for him. My daughter Jessica was next, and she was given a prescription for special herbs, crystal healing therapy, and a spiritual surgery. After I was scanned by John of God, I, too, received herbs—and a spiritual surgery!

John of God performed special spiritual surgeries for only a select group of visitors. This meant that such people were invited by the Entities to receive an invisible surgery. People who were given these surgeries sat for 5 to 20 minutes with their eyes closed, feet on the ground, and hands on their lap. They set an intention and placed their right hand on the part of their body where a healing should take place, and then they simply allowed the energies to percolate. The Entities could perform up to nine surgeries per person during a session, and the results were often astounding.

Before I was selected, I already knew that spirit had ordained this for me.

Jessica and I received an orientation that would prepare us for this special healing session the following day, and they also gave us precautions and recommendations. We were reminded that although it wasn't physical, the surgery was very much real—and even though we might not actually feel anything after the surgery, we must still treat it as one. We were also advised on how to take care of ourselves over the next 40 days in order to maximize the benefits of the surgery.

After this orientation, we were free to do whatever we wanted: from meditating with prayer around the Casa, to getting crystal healing therapy, to shopping for blessed crystal jewelry and water.

Before long, it was Thursday—the day for spiritual surgeries. Jessica and I were preparing ourselves for the session, with reminders to set our intentions, not cross anything, and sit in mindful prayer without talking either before or after the session. Our faith grew by the minute as our line proceeded to the back. My husband was sitting in meditation in the current room, but as we passed by, we didn't exchange eye contact or words, per the instructions we had been given.

As we passed John of God's empty chair, we were greeted by a woman who handed Jessica her prescription. I frowned, wondering why I hadn't received anything. However, I simply continued to follow her and the group before us. We were taken back to a dimly lit room, where we all immediately followed the spiritual operation protocol. About 15 minutes into the meditation, during which a Portuguese speaker had prayed over us, John of God came into the room. I could hear his voice praying over us as he walked up and down the aisles and released a whoosh of healing energy. His voice was powerful and deeply holy. As I sat there with my eyes closed, I simply allowed the healing energy to cascade over me, trusting that we were all receiving what we needed to better ourselves in the present and future.

About three minutes later, John of God vanished and an English voice took over, formally closing our session and inviting us all to open our eyes and exit through the rear doors. Upon exiting, we were greeted by our tour guide, who had requested the herbal prescription after realizing that mine had not been given to me. Jessica felt extremely tired, and we were both taken off to the side, where we hopped into a taxi and were escorted to our beds. We were consigned to our rooms for 24 hours without any electronics. During the 24 hours of healing, we were essentially allowing the spirit doctors to work on us. The spirit doctors were focusing on the source of our affliction, which wasn't necessarily restricted to our physical body but could be at any level of our energetic bodies. This could serve as preventative clearing when the spirits perceived someone had a disease that had not yet manifested physically.

A day later, much to my surprise, our tour guide informed me that I had once again been selected by spirit for a second spiritual surgery! This time, however, I was handed a prescription. My intuition told me that spirit knew I truly needed a second dose, particularly since my family and I were only at the Casa for a week rather than the recommended two.

After the 15 minutes of my second spiritual surgery were over, I immediately felt weak in the knees after standing up. It was almost as if I'd woken up after being given an anesthetic. I was unexpectedly groggy. Still, I had more than enough energy to thank spirit for the healing. This time, my tour guide was right outside the exit doors with a taxi, which led me straight to my bed without any words exchanged. I passed out for ten hours straight. When I came to, I had to mark the time on my calendar; I was told that after seven days post-surgery, I would welcome the entities back to remove any internal stitches with gratitude and a prayer of thanksgiving.

Another 24 hours went by, and once again, I stayed in my room. I was feeling refreshed, although tender in a few areas. I knew from how I'd been feeling that the spiritual operation had probably taken place in my abdomen, and possibly my liver and throat chakra.

After my time in "solitary confinement" passed, my husband, my daughter, and I all visited John of God's sacred healing waterfall down the road from the Casa, which we'd received permission to do. Our tour guide reminded us, "This is sacred time, but please time your healing at five minutes per person maximum. Electronics are prohibited in this area. Simply focus on the blessings being transmitted your way."

Dipping into the waterfall took our breaths away, and we all left feeling reborn and refreshed. I was utterly convinced at this point that John of God had an undeniable, God-given gift, and that spirit had brought me to him. I decided to ask to get approval to purchase one of John of God's crystal bed healing systems. I knew that the crystals had been mined from the ground beneath the surrounding land. Much to my delight, they said yes. And now, thanks to a vision that had resulted in this blessed trip in the first place, I was able to bring this special system back home with me and offer it to clients who could use healing of their own.

Finally, it was time to leave. We concluded our visit with John of God by standing in the Casa's "goodbye" line, giving thanks for all the wonderful miracles and blessings that he and his spirit doctors had given us. We had been told to bring gifts for ourselves and others so that they could be blessed by John of God, and I had the Vogel crystals with a number of water bottles in hand— ready for their next destination: home. I also purchased a number of necklaces and bracelets, as well as a poster that displayed 12 sacred saints, including a picture of John of God. I was eager to get this holy man's autograph. Without my having to say anything, he grabbed the pen and poster and initialed off on St. Francisco Javier's picture. I wasn't familiar with any of the saints in the image except John of God. I assumed that St. Francisco Javier might have been one of the Entities that performed my spiritual operation. Either way, I knew it would reveal itself in time, as I felt there was a special meaning behind this particular saint, so I treasured the gift. When I got home, I placed the poster in a frame and hung it in my healing space.

My daughter and I both felt a noticeable difference in the aftermath of our experience. Being personally blessed by John of God seemed to have prepared us for whatever was to come. We were both more energized and active, and I felt a new sense of inspiration and vitality when it came to working with energy to create healing space for others.

Months later, John of God showed up in my life once again, with a beautiful synchronicity. One day, I went to a specialty store in Calgary that sold crystals. The two owners of the shop were brothers from Brazil. One of them greeted me at the counter and said, "Long time no see!" He also remembered that I'd gone to Brazil to see John of God not long ago, so he asked me about it.

"It was quite an experience," I said, and then proceeded to tell him a bit about it. I also mentioned that I was in the process of writing my first book, and he responded by asking me if I was familiar with a particular author? I'd never heard the name before, so I asked him to repeat it.

"This guy is famous in Brazil. He's a medium who has written a number of books about his experiences and has channeled amazing information." He led me to one of the bookshelves in the shop...and much to my astonishment, the name of the author was Francisco Javier! The same name that John of God had initialed off on the picture!

As I perused the books, I realized that John of God had given me a potent message about my own life and future. I had been told by other people that the variety of writing I did was automatic, similar to trance mediums like Francisco Javier. My understanding was that John of God was simply offering me confirmation that my vision of sharing my experiences with a broad audience through my writing would be fulfilled.

To this day, the decision I made to go to Brazil with my family to see John of God is one of the best decisions I've ever made. I encourage anyone who is seeking to heal to have that experience and invest in themselves—and to surrender their well-being to spirit. No matter what Western medicine has told us about our prospects and longevity, there is always hope for us—and Divine messengers like John of God are here to strengthen our faith and our souls.

This is not to denigrate Western medicine, but to find ways to harmoniously integrate it with alternative/spiritual modalities. While doctors can observe and assess the physical body's symptoms with accuracy and precision, spiritual teachers and healers can see within and beyond.

When we are able to integrate the marvels of modern science with the deep wisdom of spirit, we learn to release our fate to the unknown consequences of infinite possibilities. We must stop fighting with ourselves and begin to observe the reactive universe, which we play a part in.

In today's society, without clarity and trust in one's mind, body and soul, we are seeing an epidemic of addiction, outrage, distorted values, and lust for power and money, all of which takes a toll on our personal health, relationships, and our societies and economies.

Surrendering is the principal key to glowing physical, mental, and spiritual health—something we rarely feel is even possible for ourselves. This surrender brings balance, harmony, bliss, and peace—and it opens portals of infinite love that we can learn to flow within. Through surrender, we can learn to align with true love and serve a purpose for all of humanity. Together, we can shine and co-create a healthier environment for our ourselves, future generations, and Mother Earth.

CHAPTER 19

A Soul-Sourced Peace Warrior

"I seek protection and sound my alarm. May body, mind, and
spirit be safe from harm. My aura a shield surrounded with
Christ's sacred light to help me stay strong, I block negativity and
release all that does not serve my highest good." —Unknown

"Therefore, let us lay aside the deeds of darkness and
put on the armour of light." —Romans 13:12

As I wrote this book, a few days after completing each chapter, I would
find myself filled with an overwhelming Christ-like presence that
washed over me—leaving me with tears of joy and a deep sense of
confirmation. Through this process, I had a number of important revelations
about the nature of illness and the wounded soul.

In cancer, the damaged soul attacks the physical body. The sick soul, which
is poisoned with hatred, doesn't care about the physical body. The only way
toward healing is to confront the sick soul with the love of God and healing
spirits.

Early in 2018, a client of mine came in to have her hair done. At the time, she
mentioned to me that the company she worked for wasn't doing too well—and
she later found she was being let go. Seeing that she and my husband worked
in the same industry, she was indecisive as to whether or not to share her loss.

Although I appreciated her obvious concern, I always try to avoid fear-based stories and to follow my gut feelings above all else. In this case, my intuition told me to end my conversation with her, and to simply send her blessings of love and light for her highest good.

Three months after returning from my visit to John of God in Brazil, I received a dream vision of my client. In this vision, I saw a series of numbers on a rotary wheel, which didn't appear to me very clearly as the wheel continued to spin. But afterwards, I received what I perceived to be a job offer. Then, my client's face popped into the vision and she asked, "Cindy, would you please pray for me?"

Upon waking up, I thought to myself, *Good, this means she's found a job!* At the same time, I was confused as to why she asked me to pray for her. I was moved to send her a message on Facebook to share what I saw, and at that point, she confirmed that she had started a new job not long ago. However, she, too, was baffled by the message in my dream in which she'd asked me to pray for her. At the end of our brief conversation, she thanked me and left it at that.

About two weeks after that message, she texted me and asked if she could call me. I responded, "Let me just clear my space, collect my thoughts, and get back to you. Can you give me five to ten minutes?"

I ended up calling her almost immediately, as I found the urgent nature of her message somewhat odd. When we talked, she broke the news to me: She had been diagnosed with breast cancer. I was shocked and saddened by this news, especially since she had a five-year-old daughter.

I immediately remembered the dream vision in which she had asked me to pray for her. I felt guided to return to those private messages and send them to her. I asked, "When did you receive your diagnosis?" It turned out that the day after sharing my dream vision, she felt an internal urge to check her breast—and sure enough, a lump was found. According to her memory, she had been receiving universal messages with the word "cancer" or overheard conversations about it everywhere she'd been a week prior to checking her breast. She went to the doctor's office two days after my dream vision—and she received the diagnosis two weeks later.

I realized that the numbers I'd seen were not related to her job offer, but to her lab tests. Her soul had reached out to me to pray for her.

I knew then and there that she had to come back to me so I could offer her a 90-minute full flushing, healing, and purification session. My sense was that spirit had led her to me for this reason alone. She agreed to come in the next day, and I was guided to make her session a priority. During the healing/clearing session, I barely laid my hands over her tumor, and she breathed in pain, which startled me.

"Are you OK? I barely touched you," I said.

She nodded. "Yes, I feel a shift, so please keep going."

I continued to pray over her and to release everything that I sensed was no longer serving her. "Divine spirit, please send a miracle on her behalf," I silently said. I innately felt that much of what needed to change was her lifestyle and her beliefs.

But it would be a miracle for her to change, I thought, without knowing how I knew this.

When her session ended, I had her sit up and handed her a glass of water so that she could collect her thoughts.

The very first words out of her mouth were, "I need to change."

My jaw dropped. I was dumbfounded but it was like music to my ears.

She also told me that she'd visualized a number of important things during our session. She said she saw that I had a Divine spiritual surgeon team, accompanied by spirit animals. At one point she saw Jesus Christ displaying his sacred heart and hovering over her at a distance. She also saw a male surgeon in a white lab coat who seemed to be assisting me. "Cindy, in my mind's eye, you looked like a wizard channeling energy from the Heavenly realm," she marveled.

A couple weeks later, my client texted me again, and I was overjoyed to read what she had to say: "I just saw my doctor. She touched me and can't find the main tumor. And the lymph node is much smaller! And the bloodwork came back great! She's so happy with the progress. Thank you."

It was amazing. The living spirit of God had just healed this woman's breast cancer in the course of a few weeks! I had told her after the first session to watch for synchronicities. I mentioned that if her chemo appointments were canceled, this meant the healing from the session was effective. And if she was led to go to an appointment, she would only need one treatment.

Although her main tumor had vanished, she ended up needing to go through one chemo treatment over six sessions. She had already shared with me that she felt she needed to undergo this process to strip away the physical layers of her body so she could be renewed and live life with a greater sense of purpose.

She had already been told by nurses and doctors that the treatment would make her feel sick, so she asked me if I could give her a 60-minute healing session the day before her first appointment, to help her prepare. Of course, I said yes. A day or so after this treatment, she sent me a selfie and shared that she felt fine. Although she was tired at times, she wasn't nauseous. I noted that she didn't even look like a cancer patient who'd just had chemo. She was beautiful, youthful, and glowing. And since then, she has only been getting better and better. My gratitude for being part of her journey, and learning from it, is deeply profound.

I sensed that my work was to be aware of the constant battle that was being waged in the invisible world around us, and that we were meant to do the work to overcome evil with good. The clearings I was doing with clients seemed to be working to increase the collective vibration and to sever karmic attachments that created illness.

There were many other instances that helped me to understand this. In the spring of 2018, I was invited to a BBQ with my husband and my youngest daughter. As the men hovered around the TV watching and betting on their favorite UFC fighters, the women hung out in the kitchen making small talk. For whatever reason, I found the energies in the space very strange, which caused me to step off to the side and detach from the scene to make sense of what I was feeling.

An acquaintance named Rhonda ended up joining the women in the kitchen. As she greeted us and reached for some appetizers, I began receiving sudden downloads about her relationship with her partner, Sean. I could see that she was feeling stagnant in her life, but she was ready to settle down and have a family. I was somewhat uncomfortable with the personal information I was receiving, so I excused myself and left to play with the kids.

Moments later, Barbara, the woman who was hosting the party, grabbed me and brought me upstairs. "Cindy, do you mind blessing my children's rooms? I'd thought of bringing in a priest to bless our home, but since you're here, I thought you could do it."

I agreed, but I was curious as to why she was requesting a blessing.

"The children have been having nightmares," she explained.

I immediately went to work clearing and blessing the three rooms without any hesitation, and I also felt guided to ask if I could lay hands over the children.

"Sure, if you can get them to!" she replied, considering that all of her kids were under the age of six.

After I felt everything was fine, it was about that time to end our gathering, as it was getting late for the little ones.

As we were saying our goodbyes, when I approached Rhonda, another insight hit me: *You have to heal her.*

I mentally responded to spirit, *I'm not going to ask her to come in for an energy healing. If she needs it, I trust you'll guide her to me in private and that she'll contact me on her own. OK? Thank you.*

It took her six weeks to acknowledge spirit's internal nudge and come to me, but one day, Rhonda sent me a message on Facebook. I knew then and there that it had to be serious. As she shared more and more information with me, I realized that my downloads had been accurate.

"Have you ever had an energy healing session before?" I asked.

"Yes, I had Reiki about two months ago."

"My type of healing offers a little twist."

She immediately said yes when I asked her if she wanted a 90-minute clearing session. In fact, she was available the next day. That night, after our conversation, I asked spirit to show me what Rhonda needed as she moved forward. Shortly after, I fell into a deep sleep, and later that night, Rhonda came to me in my dream. I was in her house, which was filled with a dark energy. Rhonda herself seemed to be filled with darkness, and the light within her almost felt as if it were held captive. She seemed restless, as if she were uncomfortable in her own body. I saw her attempting to grab her sacred angel oracle deck to do a spread, but it was surrounded by too much light, which deterred her. She became even more fidgety, but she finally gave up and placed a black tourmaline crystal atop the oracle deck to protect it from dark energy.

In the dream, she lay down so I could offer her a healing. At this time, a young girl I assumed was Rhonda's sister (because she looked just like her) appeared to the left of me and crawled into an old-fashioned toddler's bed. She began talking but her voice immediately subsided. I could still see her mouth moving, but I couldn't hear her. I looked back toward Rhonda so I could heal her. I asked her to lay down on her back, but she rolled off to her side into a fetal position. Just as I approached her, laying my hand upon her shoulder, I was attacked!

A dark and cold cloud materialized from her back; out of it, an arm and a hand formed…and then grabbed for my neck. As it began to choke me, I immediately called upon Archangel Michael. As soon as I did, the black cloud lifted—and it was gone.

I woke up feeling somewhat shaky and in the grip of the dark, hellish vibration I had experienced. But I didn't allow fear to overtake me. I quickly offered a prayer of gratitude for my Divine team. I grabbed my phone and immediately sent Rhonda a message, asking her if she had a younger sister between 10 and 13 years old, and if she lived in an old house.

She responded within minutes: "No, I don't have a younger sister. But yes, we live in an older home."

I frowned to myself. Could there be the spirit of a young girl in her home who needed to be directed to the light?

I didn't want to alarm Rhonda, so I simply told her that I'd had a vision of her in a dream and that it wasn't good. Her appointment was set for that evening, and I asked her to make sure that she arrived wearing all white.

Just as she stepped in that evening, my chest automatically became heavy. Everything behind her was dark, and I couldn't see beyond her back. As soon as she stepped in, it was if she entered a Heavenly realm that exposed what didn't belong in her aura, much like a human UV black light body scanner would. I led her into my sacred healing space for the first time. I could feel that the lower-vibration energies that surrounded her were feeling threatened.

"How are you feeling?" I asked her.

She didn't say much in response, but she seemed somewhat agitated and unsure of what to expect as she sat on the healing bed.

I then shared with her the specifics of my dream vision of what had happened, and just as I asked about the girl once again, I received a download from spirit that made me ask, "Did something bad happen to you between the ages of 10 and 13?"

She looked at me for a moment before responding, "Yes, at 13."

Before she could say anything more, I held up a hand to stop her. "You don't have to tell me anything more, but what I need you to do in this healing session is to go back and visualize yourself as that 13-year-old girl. And I need you to forgive yourself, as well as whoever was involved—and the overall situation. You need to do this in order to heal yourself in your journey."

She agreed.

"Do you believe in God?" I asked her.

"Yes, of course."

"Do you go to church?"

"No."

"That's fine. Were you ever Baptist?"

She looked at me, baffled as to why I was asking these questions. "No, why?"

"I'm just curious, but I think you should be bathed with holy water, which will protect you in future," I responded.

I asked her to lie face down on the healing bed before spiritually opening the Heavenly realms and asking them to shine over us. Given the dream I'd had, I took extra caution. Much to my amazement, I felt the same dark energy from my dream approaching my neck!

Is this really happening? I thought. And then, *If this isn't faith, then I don't know what is!*

My initial fear quickly turned to Divine courage. I was guided to grab some white sage and begin burning it in the direction of her body as she remained still. I demanded out loud that the energy move toward the crystal grid on the wall, which was surrounded by white tealight candles.

"You are not wanted here," I firmly said. "In the name of Jesus, I declare that you remove yourself from Rhonda's body!"

I could feel the crystal grid becoming a portal into the ether, sucking out the dark energy with love. I asked Rhonda if she was OK. She said yes, although she admitted she had no clue what was happening. I continued to breathe and call on my spirit team, as the energy in the room was heavy and dark, unlike anything I'd ever experienced in a waking state.

I felt the dark energy subside, and I tried to touch her shoulder a second time. I still felt some demonic attachments, but they weren't as strong this time around. "Do you know the Lord's Prayer, Rhonda?" I asked.

"No," she replied.

I laid my hands on her and began reciting the Lord's Prayer, but I found that I couldn't finish, as my throat chakra was being constricted. Once again, I asked the dark energy to leave her body and never return again. I could feel energetic layers holding Rhonda down. I began clearing the energy in her back and moving it toward the grid. As I continued, she admitted to me that she already felt lighter and more comfortable. We ended her session with John of God's crystal healing therapy, during which she fell into a deep sleep. I just smiled as she snored away. She probably hadn't slept this well in a long time. I prayed over her during this time, intending for the three wishes she had come in with to be brought to fruition and for the universe to help her navigate her journey.

When she woke up, she once again confirmed that she felt lighter after her session. "Thank you for saving my life," she said softly.

I advised her to go home with the white sage bundle I'd used during her session and to sage everything in her house, including her partner. As I followed her outside to sage her vehicle, I received another insight from spirit: *Rhonda was suicidal.*

I immediately looked at her and asked, "Were you suicidal?"

She nodded sadly. "Yes, and that's why I thanked you for saving my life."

I smiled at her. "You will never feel that way again. If you honor your soul by investing in your internal healing and happiness, you will intuitively be led by your angels." I also suggested that she keep an eye on how her partner behaved around her, as I intuited that he, too, could use a healing.

The following day, Rhonda told me that her partner had complained about the sage scent that she'd filled the home with, which for me, was a clear sign that he needed healing. A couple days later, they both came to me. I put him on the healing bed as Rhonda observed from the side. He admitted to me during the session that he felt a sense of distance from God, so I had him visualize himself as a pure young boy throughout the healing. Throughout the session, I could smell his fear. As I placed my hand on his head, he began to sweat profusely. I knew he had the same attachments as Rhonda, and so I went through the same motions as I had during her session. By the time his session ended, his sensitivity to the sage was gone, and I didn't need a towel to wipe up his sweat.

After that, Rhonda messaged me with thanks for intervening on their behalf.

All of my experiences with clients and out in the world have helped me to understand that I'm a warrior of pure love, making peace with the light energies of God to help keep away all lower attachments that no longer serve people.

Ultimately, by choosing a lower-vibrational lifestyle, we are creating an invitation to negative energies who then manipulate us for their own dark purposes. This can leave us desensitized to their violence and can even bring on self-victimization and suicidal thoughts. In this time, there are a number of "lost souls" out there that feel confused, alone, and stagnant. Many of them are being attacked by negative energies without their knowledge. Like leeches, these energies are drawn to people, nations, and all those who are lost. The increased rate of suicides and mental health issues among young people demonstrates that many of these energetic attachments are taking hold of us.

Just as there is light, there is darkness; so whether we like it or not, these lower energies exist. I say this not to instigate fear, but to increase the awareness that we must protect ourselves rather than succumb to their power. We can lovingly and firmly ask these energies to leave us, and to be released to God's light.

Every single one of us is a sacred channel with the power to access darkness or light through our free will. Our creator offers Heavenly portals that open to help us in our time of need.

John of God has shared that it can be difficult for healing energies to enter lower-vibrational planes that we may find ourselves in, so the process of maintaining a high vibration is so important. I generally tell my clients that they must perform their own post-treatment so that they can open up to greater healing. Sadly, many of them don't follow simple advice about making lasting changes to their lifestyles, because this requires personal transformation.

However, for the most part, I have witnessed a huge transformation in most of them. Many of my clients become healthier, more active, and more loving. The truth is, once they agree to a healing session, there will always be a positive outcome, whether they see it or not.

I also understand that often, diseases are necessary and can even keep us from creating more serious illnesses or negative karmic consequences that keep us stuck in spiritual pain in this life, as well as future lives. Despite pain and suffering, we can experience great love and endurance, which offer us vital medicine for spiritual recovery.

For my part, I know that I will continue to keep following the revelations of the Heavenly kingdom. I will continue to honor what I have been commanded to do on my journey. I will continue to help change the lives of God's people, who are each individually the bodies of Christ.

CHAPTER 20

Believe in the Freedom of Love

"Our deepest fear is not that we are inadequate. Our deepest fear is that we are powerful beyond measure. It is our light, not our darkness, that most frightens us. We ask ourselves, 'Who am I to be brilliant, gorgeous, talented and fabulous?' You are a child of God. Your playing small does not serve the world. There's nothing enlightened about shrinking so that other people won't feel insecure around you. We are born to make manifest the glory of God that is within us; it's in everyone. And as we let our own light shine, we unconsciously give other people permission to do the same. As we are liberated from our own fear, our presence automatically liberates others."—Marianne Williamson

"Heaven and earth shall pass away but my words
shall not pass away." —*Matthew 24:35*

Thank you for allowing me to share my journey as an open book. Over the last year, I've used the stories, parables, and prophetic experiences of my own journey to emphasize one thing: It doesn't matter what religion you practice, for all religions carry some truth about our fundamental nature of infinite love. I have concluded that God is greater than all religions and that there is no religion in Heaven but a simple worship of His presence daily. Whatever religion resonates with your soul is the right one. There is no need to chase after Him but to seek Him within our sacred hearts.

As long as you are connected to some belief in a higher power that is full of truth, unconditional love, and unity, you will be able to integrate the lessons I have shared with you. The lesson I most wish to convey is that it's so important to intuitively listen with an open heart and mind to what the universe is showing us, for this is the direction we should heed, respect, and follow.

Those who attend church for the sake of reading scripture and following fear-based commands are limiting themselves from feeling the full vibration of love. They are merely touching the surface. Once they can shed their separation-based ego, and swallow their pride, they will plunge into the ocean of God consciousness and rise up to meet the almighty power of guidance, authentically, as seekers of truth. Curiosity about this higher presence will bring new meaning to their existence on this planet that a routine church mass will not offer alone. Divine intelligence is within and all around us.

His love exceeds all boundaries, and it is up to us as to how we will spend our energy of free will. At the end of our life, we will better understand the consequences of our actions and whether or not we were able to move with the universal flow versus our ego, during our life review. We will also reflect on how we could've been nicer to ourselves, or removed our focus from our egos to help others and aid in the evolution of society.

We need not continue to accrue the karma of our past events by repeating hardships and lessons. In this life, we can evolve and prepare ourselves for the next cycle of life. God, His universe, and our soul always lead us with unseen compassion, wisdom, and understanding. With the help of Divine light and clarity that comes from personal healing, we can come together to co-create universal healing from which we can all benefit, and that can help future generations to come.

Speaking of future generations, how many of us have children? Or have been a child once? I'm sure you will agree based on your own upbringing that it's crucial to be aware that we need to be supportive of our children's soulful desires and decisions, as well as their God-given gifts and passions. This will save us and our planet. We as parents need to accommodate ourselves to their soul growth, not our ego's desires for them.

Children born in these generations and ones to come will be highly gifted with abilities that will aid them in soul-driven missions much greater than we can imagine. It's happening around us as you read this. We are seeing infant prodigies and "indigo children" who remember their past lives. So when we make the decision to have children, we must invest in them while also nourishing our own soul purpose and caring for the inner child within, which is integral to deep healing. After all, for so many adults, their inner children are shut down by the contracts we make with society. This is how we lose access to our powerful inner world.

It would be ideal to incorporate meditation in schools across the world, and even in doctors' offices! In case you haven't noticed, our earth is crying out and so are our people—no matter what pay-grade level we're at or which car we drive. We are in transitional times, and tuning into subliminal universal messages will help us to prepare for the radical changes occurring in and around us.

How many of us feel as if our structures of reality are collapsing, while new ones are emerging? For many, this is creating confusion and disorientation, as well as feelings of helplessness. Be aware that this is the season during which anything holding us down in the lower vibrations will fall away as we evolve into higher vibrations. It is our decision as to whether we will stubbornly hold on with our egos flailing in the midst of change...or whether we will surrender to grace and let go.

Now is a good time to release old patterns that do not serve you, including negative emotions and habits. Cultivate the clear intention to let go and embrace the fifth dimension.

There is so much noise in the world playing out—from the 24/7 news cycle to politics to the excessive lifestyles we see on television or the Internet. All of it can be deceiving to our physical eyes and contaminate our minds. Watching too much television that doesn't have meaning detracts from our energy levels and can get us all riled up, which may cause us to lose sleep over events we have no control over. The lack of sleep and the growth of external illusions can eat away at us and contaminate our thoughts. It's vital to watch how you're spending your energy, especially in your free time. Self-love should always be at the top of your recreational list.

Today, more and more people are being Divinely guided and are experiencing unexpected awakenings. Through my intuitive formula—claircognizance (clear knowing) + clairsentience (clear feeling)—mixed with research, I know that it is estimated that in approximately a couple decades, a whole new reality of the golden age (also known as the New Earth) will prevail. In this reality, all people will be living in peace and harmony with all life, fully respecting humanity and earth itself. Unconditional love and compassion will overflow, and so will equality and justice. Poverty, hunger and crime will be extinct. Abundance will be available to all. We will be living in Heaven on earth.

So even when you feel resistant to change, it is important to move with the flow of life and be more playful and curious with your perceptions of reality. We can practice trusting our intuition more and following our true paths so that we may co-create with the universe and usher in a new age.

Over the years, we have been destroying this planet, and in most cases, each other in return, perpetuating on the environment what we are doing to ourselves. But the Old Earth is being separated into the New Earth, and has been ever since the shift in 2012. We are entering new dimensions, which is raising the vibrations and frequencies of our planet and giving rise to the greatest show on earth, literally! When the separation is complete, the Old Earth will be left behind with all its negativity and chaos, while those who have raised the vibrations and frequencies of their bodies will enter the New Earth, which will be the paradise that Biblical scripture predicted long ago.

The signs that you are shifting might seem alarming. With the rise in frequencies, you might also experience depression, heart palpitations, high blood pressure, and joint aches—and once your doctor has no explanation as to why you are feeling these symptoms, you will intuitively know why they are occurring. Those who are ready, willing, and open will be part of the New Earth. They will be reassured that the symptoms are going to be short-lived before they level off. It is all part of the transition.

There are simple things we can do to prepare. We can watch our diets by staying away from heavy red meats (unless you are a blood type O negative, which tends to mean you have an iron deficiency) and sugar. We can eat lighter, cleaner foods that don't weigh us down. When we do this, we will notice the shift. We will also become more consciously aware of the fact that we are not craving the foods that we used to eat. Ideal foods include fresh fruits, vegetables, and sustainably harvested seafood, as well as liquids (preferably alkaline water)—all foods that I avoided until my teens. Your spiritual body will nudge you if you take the time to simply listen to and honor your body and what it is telling you.

As the two worlds are separating and taking place, as stated in the Book of Revelations, sadly, those who are left behind will be the ones caught in a negative and destructive state, wherein they've allowed their greed and illusions of separation to dictate their reality. They have resisted the transformation and are stuck in a dense karmic state such that they will remain on the Old Earth, then reincarnating into other star systems until the karmic debt has been repaid. At that point, they will be able to enter the New Earth—if they ever so choose to.

Upon awakening, I was not given all this information by the teachers I encountered early on. So I am happy to have cultivated this knowledge over years of study and meditation, and to share it with you now. Those who are still in a slumbering stage may have difficulty raising their frequency quickly enough—so if this is the case, they should allow it to happen gradually and in an unforced way. Those who have recently awakened simply got there early and need only stay attuned, calm, and humble, continuing to live in a space of God consciousness.

There is no need to panic, but to simply and eagerly experience our own evolution. Another thing to keep in mind is that we live in the energies of Divine order; that is, we are not supposed to go out and change anyone but to be here in support of one another, enlightened or not. We must allow everyone we encounter, even our close loved ones, to find their own way. Our job is to merely shed light on the freedom of love within this universe.

The shape this earth is in cannot be reversed. The only way to save the earth is for God and our collective to co-create a new one. Sadly, humanity has destroyed civilizations through time and has misused the power of free will. By choosing to develop our psychic powers, we can bring forth positive changes to better hone our navigation systems and support others in doing the same. Our soul mission comes down to believing in the era we were born in during this lifetime, resetting our system, unlearning fear, believing in the freedom of love, raising awareness and consciousness of the world, and healing in the process.

The impossible is our ultimate reality. And the only reality is in the now. As we are present with each heartbeat, we experience the flow of life's grace.

Watching the clock as time passes by, we know we are all on borrowed time... and each second, minute, and season is an opportunity for internal growth.

Souls come and go beyond dimensions here and there, as each one evolves on their own. Many of us may have experienced an inexplicable homesickness, a sense of missing the unknown that rests at our very core, moving into and throughout the threads of our heart.

Take comfort in this vast cosmos, which is the source of so much peace, healing, joy, and love. For this is not our home. Eternity is and forever will be our true resting place.

ACKNOWLEDGEMENTS

I want to give all my appreciation and honor to God, our Divine creator, for your unconditional love, intervention, compassion, peace, guidance, protection, and the healings that you have shown me firsthand. Without your Divine power through my guides intervening on my behalf in 1981 and again in 2014, none of this would have been possible. The results yielded are rewarding enough. Because I know you hear me, I surrender and release this book to you in spirit on your behalf and know that you will do great things through the healing energies of these words given.

I am grateful for the universal nudge that led me to be personally blessed by John of God and the selfless Entities that were incorporated with the purpose of healing, and preparing me and others to offer our own healing energies; in return, I acknowledge the Divine spirit that dwells in each human being.

I also want to thank Mother Mary, my earth dad, my brother, and my step-father, all of whom are family in spirit. I also thank my ancestors, as well as my spiritual healing team for your synergistic feminine and masculine energies, which help bring balance. Thank you all for having my back, choosing to accompany me through this life journey, and facilitating the healings in my life. Your support beyond the veil speaks for itself.

To my friends, clients, acquaintances, and companions who allowed me to share their personal healing testimonials—thank you for bringing hope to others. You know who you are. This is a Divine gift that keeps on giving, from my heart to yours.

I want to give immense thanks to my editor, Nirmala Nataraj, for her dedication and patience, and for helping me better understand the writing process, sharing my vision, and giving me a voice that I never had. My gratitude is beyond words.

A warm, heartfelt thanks to my husband for investing in me by choosing to put a ring on it ten years ago and keeping up with all my spontaneous spiritual adventures and projects these past four. You are like a dragon who observes in the distance! I love you!

I want to thank my beautiful daughters—Jasmine, Jade, and Jessica—for choosing me to be their mom in this lifetime. Keep living an intuitive lifestyle to its fullest just the way you are. To Jade, I personally thank you for flowing through this process alongside me. I am blessed to have you all in my life and only want the best for each of you. If you are happy, I am happy! Lastly, always remember that no matter where life may take us, I am always with you in spirit and just a thought away.

A special thanks to my grandchildren, Aaliyah and Gabriel, for being such wonderful blessings to me. Your great-grandpa in spirit was so right about you two. You both gave me such motivation to keep going with this project with your constant entertainment. Thank you for keeping me young at heart. Please always remember to follow your spirit and speak from your soul. Also, don't forget to thank your mommy for all her hard work and dedication!

To my family: Being a spiritual healer by day and a prophetic dreamer by night has had its fair share of adversity. People are often afraid of what they don't understand; therefore, misunderstandings about where I have been spiritually guided and who I am today can run rampant. Regardless, all of this helps me better understand myself and how to not take people, places, or things too seriously (even if they are family). We are all living as temporary characters here—I have chosen to make the most of it by honoring my soul and investing in myself, but most importantly, being a witness to the reunion of eternal love in others. It's time to mend our family circle by letting down our guards respectfully, and making a conscious effort to resolve our differences by supporting one another as we reunite with our door keepers and watchers—just as our noble ancestors once did. Forgiveness starts within.

In order to succeed, we must believe in ourselves. May we never allow the lower energies to defame God our creator's abundance among mankind.

ABOUT THE AUTHOR

Cindy Simpson Jurado is a First Nations Christian mystic. Although she was raised in a broken family and often felt undervalued, shut down, and without a voice, her story is a testament to the power of Divine love.

At the age of five, Cindy's spirit entered her physical body for the very first time; upon that realization, she was immediately given a fatal medical diagnosis of life-threatening asthma. Cindy's mother, a First Nations residential school survivor, couldn't stand the thought of losing her daughter and felt guided to return to her ancestral ways by introducing her to a Divine intervention in the form of laying of hands, which miraculously healed Cindy's asthma and changed her life.

In 2014, Cindy underwent a spiritual awakening after three of her family members transitioned into the spirit world within a year of one another. A Divine force led her to surrender to her soul's greater calling. When she received the insight to be baptized, her spiritual gifts were catalyzed and she discovered her capacity for healing, prophecy, and tapping into energies that were not her own. Many of her subsequent experiences have been decidedly "supernatural" and have offered Cindy vivid visions about multiple dimensions, spiritual warfare, and the New Earth—as well as experiences of deep healing. She prefers not to take any credit for each miraculous healing but would much rather have her client show respect and gratitude to God the creator. Cindy wants to be remembered and valued for her acts of kindness, compassion, and being of service.

As a prophetic dreamer, she often finds herself healing others through her sleep; by day, she is a spiritual intercessor in partnership with God's living spirit and her own surgical spirit team. Through her healing business, Soul Sanctuary Blessings, Cindy works with clients in search of healing and a sense of deeper meaning and purpose. Cindy's clients often describe her as compassionate, adventurous, inspiring, and someone who always speaks her truth. As an empath and a certified Hospital Unit Clerk (HUC), Cindy is adept at connecting with a variety of different people and issues. Cindy's miracles include healing breast cancer, infertility, childhood trauma, psychological problems, and rare non-curable physical disorders.

Cindy wrote this book in partnership with the Divine through automatic writing. Her intention to uplift others by inviting awareness that contributes to their own healing, as well as offering them a glimpse of how we can move through the challenges of our lives with faith, love, hope, internal strength, and a spirit of self-discovery. She hopes to remind everyone that we are always surrounded with extra help in the form of sacred beings, Heavenly portals, and the potential for miraculous spiritual awakening.

Cindy is a proud mom of three daughters, a grandmother of two radiant children, and a devoted wife. She lives in Calgary, Canada, with her husband and two younger daughters.

Made in the
USA
Middletown, DE